HAVING IT ALL

HAVING IT ALL

A PRACTICAL GUIDE TO OVERCOMING THE CAREER WOMAN'S BLUES

BY

Joyce Gabriel
AND
Bettye Baldwin

M. EVANS and Company, Inc.
NEW YORK

Library of Congress Cataloging in Publication Data

Gabriel, Joyce.
  Having it all.

   1. Women—Psychology. 2. Success. 3. Self-
actualization (Psychology). 4. Women—Employment.
I. Baldwin, Bettye, joint author. II. Title.
HQ1221.G22   301.41′2   79-23283
ISBN 0-87131-302-2

M. Evans and Company, Inc.
216 East 49 Street
New York, New York 10017

Design by Robert Bull

Manufactured in the United States of America

9 8 7 6 5 4 3 2 1

To all Career Women,
and especially to those
who shared their stories with us

CONTENTS

ONE

HAVING
IT ALL

I wake up in the morning, and I feel as if the whole world is open to me. I'm in control of my life. I have a job that I love, a man I love who loves me and is supportive, friends who nurture me, and the money I need to create the lifestyle I want.

Writing my second book is the most liberating thing that has ever happened to me. I'm finally doing now—in my sixties—what I thought for years only other people could do. I'm making enough money to do things for my children and grandchildren. After two marriages that were a mistake, I've realized that living alone gives me the most pleasure and freedom. My only regret is that I didn't realize sooner that I could live my life this way.

I feel totally in control of my life, with unlimited options. Because of my MBA and work experience, people seek me out for jobs. Because I've managed my money well, I'm financially independent enough to take time out from my business life to go back to school for my doctorate. I've traveled all over the world, and because I've chosen to remain single, I don't have to answer to anyone but me. When I want a change, I put my few possessions into storage and move into a new life. I have a network of friends around the country. My life is pretty full, except that sometimes I miss the companionship and commitment of a love relationship. In fact, now that I'm in my thirties, I'm making finding Mr. Right the top priority. I never thought I'd say it, but I'm ready to settle down.

THE QUOTES ARE from three career women of different ages, from different backgrounds. Their values and attitudes vary, but they share one basic motivation that underscores everything they do: They're determined to have it all.

Having it all is what this book is about. As career women we have discovered the joys of working at purposeful, powerful, often glamorous and lucrative jobs. But we've also discovered that a successful career by itself is not enough. We want our personal lives to be equally rewarding, equally fulfilling. And we've seen that we need to gain control of the personal sphere of our lives in the same way we've taken command of the professional sphere.

What we've written is a how-to book, a practical guide to overcoming any problems or obstacles that career women may face, to achieve a well-balanced, integrated, joyful way of life. We don't intend to minimize the problems, the obstacles, and the juggling all of us do every day of our lives. But we don't intend to moan about these either. Women today are in the options market. For the first time in history, we can choose the kinds of lives we want. If a career is part of it, then all of us must recognize that we'll pay a certain price, as men have done for centuries, by having a split focus: on ourselves as private people and as business people.

We've all read the books about how to make it in a man's world, how to learn the business games mother never taught us, how to dress for success, manipulate through gamesmanship, and win big in business. But nowhere have we seen career women addressed as people, with all the human needs they had before they were "liberated" from their homes, allowing us to go out into the world of work. Now that we no longer have to choose between career and marriage, between career and having a family, how do we manage to have them all?

We'll warn you at the outset that there are no easy answers, no simple formulas for learning how to get what you want in all areas of your life. What do exist are principles, guidelines, approaches, and strategies that have worked for us and can work for you. We have twenty-eight years of combined career experience to draw from. Out of those experiences, we've developed methods for approaching life that help sort out what's important from what isn't, help you focus on the important things and bring your life into balance. Beyond our valuable combined experience, there are other women, with different experiences, who have their own ideas and experiences to share. We interviewed many of them for this book. Some are married, some single; some have children, some don't. Like the three women whose comments begin this book, they all want to have it all, and any nuggets of wisdom they've shared with us we'll share with you.

We'll talk about how to develop yourself as an independent, self-starting person, how to separate yourself from your job, how to make and maintain friendships with people of both sexes, how to have a successful marriage when both of you have careers. We'll look at children as part of having it all, help you decide whether you want them and when you should have them, in terms of your marriage and your career, and how you can manage the dual career of being a mother and a businesswoman. We'll talk about money and how you can control it because money means power, options, and control of your life. We'll discuss moving out on your own, away from the corporate structure and into your own business. We'll help you decide whether this is the right career path for you and, if it is, tell you how you can make it work. We'll talk about the fine art of sharing with your spouse, whether and how you should relocate for your career. We'll help you cope with change in your life, positive and negative. We'll talk about the importance of an Old Girls' Network and how to plug into an existing one or start one of your own. We'll discuss crises—from getting fired to the loss of a loved one—and how to survive them. Finally, we'll talk about the Career Woman's Blues and how to beat them.

We'll share our experiences and those of the women we interviewed, through personal anecdotes and quotes. We've provided charts, checklists, and quizzes to help you make decisions in important areas of your life, from how to choose the right man to how to manage your money.

We'll tell you how you can be the prime mover in all areas of your life, gaining control and getting what you want, not through manipulation, but through thought, planning, and effort.

The Power—and Problems—of Choice

Today women can integrate their lives, choosing the elements that suit them and bring them pleasure. They can choose to remain single without being called old maids. They can choose to have careers and earn their place in the business world. They can choose to live with a man, or marry a man, and continue working. They can choose to have children or not. They can combine bringing up a family with building a career.

They can choose a lifestyle—urban, suburban, formal, or informal. They can hire people and services to do much of the routine work for them—cooking, cleaning, laundry, you name it.

The secret is to find the winning combination for you, to establish a life plan and make it work. It takes organization of time, money, and resources. It takes planning, imagination, and a sense of humor. And it takes courage because each woman has to choose for herself what path to take. Each path will probably involve some problem solving to make it work.

Four years ago Rebecca was in an unhappy marriage, tucked away in a wealthy suburb with a young daughter to rear and nothing else to call her own. She knew she had problems. "All through my twenties, when people talked to me, there was nobody home. I just didn't exist, except in relation to other people. I thought a husband and a child would fulfill me. But nothing could fulfill me because I hadn't bothered to find out who I was or what I wanted."

Her first step was to admit to herself that she was unhappy. She worked with a psychiatrist to sort out her problems and find out what she wanted to do with her life. Then she took action. She got a divorce and custody of her daughter. She began to do some free-lance writing for the local newspaper and took a job for a brief time as a magazine editor to supplement her income. She hired a young woman to live in and help with the cooking and housework and with looking after her daughter, Susan. And she began to date.

A year after her divorce she met Sam and, after dating him for several months, knew that she wanted to marry him. But she knew that Sam would have to accept Susan as part of her life.

"I told him," she said, "that Susan and I are a package deal. Love me, love my kid."

Sam was more than willing to extend his love to both of them, but Susan had doubts. As Rebecca relates it, "I sat Susan down and talked to her like an adult. I said, 'Marrying Sam will make me very happy. If I am happy, you'll be happier. And if I don't marry Sam because you don't want me to, I'll be miserable, and that will make you miserable. In a few years you'll have a life of your own, independent of me, but right now I'm making this decision for our lives.' "

Today the three of them (plus two dogs) are living happily in a rural setting that gives Rebecca the quiet and freedom to write, yet is within commuting distance of Sam's photography studio. Rebecca has a column in the local newspaper and is working on her first book. At forty, her life is "overflowing with happiness."

Rebecca gambled on the things she wanted in her life. She took a risk by telling Sam and Susan, the two people most important to her, what she needed to make her life work. Because she was strong in her own decisions, all of them ended up having what they wanted. She had the courage to follow through on the life plan she had chosen.

When we decided to write this book, we knew we didn't have all the answers. What we did have were the right questions and some truths born of experience. We also had tremendous resources in the women we know who are coping with the same issues we wanted to explore, combining careers with relationships, family, children, friends—all the things that make us whole, happy, sane people. We felt that by sharing our experiences, and those of other career women, we could show women the way to having it all.

Perhaps the most important principle we can share with you is that having it all is a *process*. No one suddenly wakes up one morning to the perfect life. And a life that has been brought into balance can go out of balance for a period of time—through death, divorce, a job change or relocation, an illness, getting fired, whatever. What we've found separates those who succeed from those who don't is persistence in the face of setbacks or problems. After all, life is a series of challenges. The people who rise to the challenges generally survive and prosper. And usually you can learn something from every new experience even if it's a crisis.

In the year before this book was begun, we both had gone through incredible changes in our personal and professional lives. Bettye had gotten divorced, had a child, moved to Mexico to begin a new job, remarried, and returned to New York to work for a new company.

She had become pregnant just as her marriage was falling apart. She decided to separate from her husband, but she wanted to have her child. This was a conscious decision, made after she had carefully weighed all the changes in her life that having a child would mean. And she wanted to continue her career in the personnel department of a multinational bank.

As a single pregnant woman Bettye worked at not feeling sorry for herself. She kept herself busy with friends who were supportive and weeded out those who wanted to tell her what a mistake she was making.

She made sure that she remained as effective on her job as she had been before the pregnancy. When she was offered a job in Mexico City as personnel manager for the bank, she accepted. She gave birth to her daughter, Ashley, in Shreveport, Louisiana, where a long-time supportive friend saw her through the delivery. A month after Ashley was born, Bettye was back at work. She hired a nurse for Ashley, rented a house in Mexico City, and immersed herself in her new job and her new family.

During that year in Mexico a man who had been a friend at the bank in New York began visiting Bettye in Mexico. Within a year they decided to marry. Bettye received a job offer to become director of corporate recruiting and personnel administration for a major cosmetics company based in New York. Since her husband Charlie's career was in New York, she closed up the house and returned there with Ashley.

Bettye managed to relocate, remarry, and make an upward move in her career within eighteen months after she became a mother.

Joyce had relocated to Ohio to become lifestyles editor of a major newspaper. She left behind in New York the man she had loved for four years to take a better job opportunity. They agreed to see how things would work out. The first few months in a strange city, hundreds of miles from home, were lonely. She spent a lot of time and money on long-distance phone calls and visits to New York on weekends. She and Peter saw each other about once a month.

Six months after she moved to Ohio, two major things happened: Joyce won a national award for the lifestyes section she edited, and she and Peter became engaged, without knowing who would relocate for whom.

Peter was willing to interview in Ohio, and together they made contact with companies and search firms that would be able to place him in his field.

For six months they planned a life in Ohio until Peter was offered the advertising directorship of a major New York newspaper. He took the job and decided wedding plans would have to wait. Even if Joyce was willing to relocate to New York immediately, he didn't feel he could start a new, demanding job and a marriage at the same time. The engagement was off.

Joyce felt completely disoriented. The job in Ohio had turned into a dead end. She had accomplished all she could accomplish there. The man she had planned to marry was at least temporarily unavailable. She decide to make plans of her own. She made the decision to leave Ohio and either return to New York or relocate to one of several cities where jobs had been offered.

In the end, her decision to return to New York was a personal and professional one. The job in international public relations offered her by a major cosmetics company was intriguing. And she had discovered that, although she had formed wonderful friendships during her year in Ohio, the people she loved—family and friends—were in New York. The time was right to go home.

Returning to New York gave Joyce and Peter an opportunity to see each other again and to take a second look at their relationship. A year after Joyce returned to New York, they were married.

That was a year of challenge and growth for both of us. We found that we both came away with more confidence in our ability to cope as women on our own, while keeping our careers going in the right direction.

Learning to Be Responsible for Our Own Lives

One day, as we were discussing what had happened to us in that one-year period, we realized that we had grappled with the major challenge facing women today: to be in control of our lives no matter what happens. Neither one of us had ever wanted to be one-dimensional workaholics. We had always wanted rich lives filled with good friends and a man to love, as well as a career. Yet we had always remained highly ambitious and dedicated to our work.

We know it isn't always easy to keep a career moving forward while keeping personal lives together. And we know that in the work environment, for the most part, no one cares to know how we manage to juggle the elements of our lives. Job performance is—and should be—the bottom line. It's up to us to organize the rest. We need to take responsibility for our own lives.

The business world is not a nurturing parent. We've discovered any support we receive comes from within ourselves, from our husbands and friends, and from other women going through the same experiences. Mostly, we've taken a commonsense approach to all aspects of our lives, correcting the mistakes and capitalizing on the successes.

Using Ourselves as Role Models

As more and more women establish themselves in careers, we need to look to ourselves—and to other successful women—for role models. Viewing men as role models just doesn't work unless we can learn from their mistakes. Culturally men have been taught that work is the most important aspect of their lives. Many men have buried themselves in their work, becoming workaholics. (It's interesting to note that as more women begin careers, some of them have joined the workaholic ranks, too. Obviously they've chosen to emulate the wrong attitudes of their male colleagues.) Wives and children are often compartmentalized to fit into a corner of their lives—moving them out to the suburbs helps. For most men, there is no connection between their business lives and their "real" lives.

On the job, men keep emotions tightly under control. The macho man appears to have no feelings. But the stress, tension, and frustration have to go somewhere. He either takes his bad feelings home with him, to vent on his family, or keeps them bottled up inside to form an ulcer or explode in a heart attack. He may even have an extra drink or two at lunch or after work to make him "feel better."

In most cases, his social life is determined by his wife. She plans weekends or evenings with friends which he attends or participates in, but he rarely initiates social encounters.

Culturally, too, a man has had very little choice about whether or not he works. Until recently the man was almost always the sole support of his family. If a wife accused her husband of working his life away at the expense of spending time with his family, he would most likely respond, "Do you think I work because I like it? I work to provide all this," accompanied with hand gestures to include the house, the car, even the food on the table and the clothes on his children.

Because more than half the women in America are working today, both sexes have more options in what they choose to work at and how many hours of the day they need to devote to that work. Women can teach men to approach work as an option, as a productive occupation that can be rewarding without being all-consuming. Women may be able to teach men to live, not as chairmen of the board or macho men, but as people.

Women have traditionally been more emotional than men because they have been allowed to be. Little girls are taught they can be vulnerable, that they can have feelings. As little girls grow into women, they retain the capacity to feel empathy and compassion that can bring a human quality into the work environment. Men can learn from women that you can feel things without falling apart.

Women have been taught to be nurturing and supportive. Frequently these qualities make for the kinds of managers who can understand people and motivate them to perform in a positive way, rather than through fear or intimidation.

If we can bring these qualities of emotional openness and vulnerability, of support and nurturing into the working world, we can change the business environment in a major way.

By showing men how to combine a business life with a personal life, we can enrich all our lives. But we know that if women are to lead the business world in a new direction, they'll have to do it by conscious choice.

One of the saddest things we've seen is the women who try to succeed in business by mindlessly imitating men: the women with "brass balls" who can be "tough." Sometimes, of course, those descriptions are used to malign women who are merely being (properly) assertive. But there are women out there who want to be one of the boys, who want to live their lives as men have lived theirs and who think, as many men do, that to be strong you have to be tough.

If we consciously choose the qualities we want to incorporate from the way men function in business, we can benefit tremendously from their experience without repeating their mistakes.

For example, men have been taught to function well in groups, as a team, through team sports. Women have been taught to be competitive with other women. In most business situations, cooperative, joint effort is needed. Women can successfully incorporate team playing into their corporate behavior.

Men have learned to be decisive in business. Women have been taught to follow someone else's lead, and as a consequence, when placed in decision-making positions, they frequently tend to be indecisive. Part of gaining control of our lives is the ability to make decisions, perhaps even several at once, without hesitation.

What we need to construct is a new kind of business person. And as women enter the work force in ever greater numbers, our influence can be tremendous.

Life Begins with Self-Awareness

Before we can conquer the world, we need to know ourselves. You won't be successful in life unless you start out with a firm base, and that base is *you*. Culturally women have been brought up to be reactors—they react to their fathers, their husbands, their children—but they weren't taught to be initiators of action. Yet, to gain control of your own life and make it work for you, you need to set goals and initiate action. And before you can do that, you need to know who you are and what you really want.

To begin, strip away the cultural myths that can trap, frustrate, anger, and, if you're not aware of them, stop you. Once you've identified these, you can be rid of them—cheerfully, assertively, and confidently. If mother always told you to stay home and have babies, and that was it for fulfillment, you need to evaluate those values for yourself by asking, "Is that what I want to do with my life?" If it is, fine. But if it isn't, you need to set other goals for yourself, determined by your own values.

A career as a magazine editor was the last thing Judy's father had in mind for her. From an ethnic background that decreed woman's place was in the home, he wanted his daughter to become a secretary, who would work until she got married. A good marriage, of course, was the ultimate goal, the mark of being a successful woman.

Judy had other ideas. She worked days to help support herself and her family and attended night college, where she also edited the college newspaper, something of which her father did not approve.

"Even though I knew my father was dying, I told him that I wouldn't give up editing the newspaper," Judy explains. "It was a difficult decision to make at a fairly tender age—I was still in my teens at the time. As far as my father was concerned, my greatest aspiration should have been to graduate from Katharine Gibbs secretarial school. But I made my own choice, knowing that it would hurt him and that he'd never approve. I'd decided I wanted a career in journalism, and I was determined to pursue it."

Through a lead from a relative, Judy landed a job at a women's magazine after her father died and there was no more money for college. She began as secretary to the editor and then started writing "back of the book" features (short service stories). She also began to do free-lance writing and eventually was offered a job as fashion editor of a major magazine. Had she waited for papa's approval, she would never have had the career she wanted.

It's your life. Nobody is going to care more about you than *yourself*. If you choose a course, you need the courage to follow through, even if no one else approves your choice. In order to choose a course, you need to know what you want to do; in order to have the courage to pursue it, you need to have confidence in your ability to make judgments about what's right for your life.

If you were taught that women have to be subservient, or dumb, or nonambitious, or noncompetitive, you need to check these premises and resolve them in your own mind. Ignoring them won't make them go away; it will just make it impossible for you to be successful and *enjoy* your success. And enjoying your success is important. After all, what's the struggle for, if not for happiness and a better life?

Choosing Your Goals and Sticking to Them

To break free of all the old notions, a woman needs to be independent enough to set her own goals. It can be scary at first, but in the end, each of us is responsible for her own life, and having it all requires having yourself as the ultimate authority for the actions you'll take.

Everything you do needs to become your choice. And that doesn't mean being selfish or ruthless. For example, if you decide to have children, then spending most or all of your free time with them is your choice, not a chore imposed on you. If you choose to have a career of your own, and you marry a man who also has a career, then you at least have to consider the possibility of job relocation offers for one or both of you and decide who moves for whom and under what circumstances. Sure, they're tough decisions, but the business world is the big leagues (to use one of the men's favorite sports metaphors), and, if you want a career, you have to Pay to Play, one of our basic principles of learning to make trade-offs, which we'll expand on in Chapter Two. Having it all does not mean being able to pursue any whim; you continually have to make responsible choices.

There will be times when you'll have to fight for your right to responsible choice. For example, if you choose to combine a career with having a family, don't let your boss determine whether you can work and bring up children. That's your choice. Nor should being a working mother make you ineligible for a promotion. After all, working fathers are promoted all the time.

Responsible choice also takes courage. Being a career woman does not mean being a superwoman. You don't have to prove anything to anyone, including peers who want to test your woman power. If you're offered a great job with a great salary, but the job happens to be in Toledo, Ohio, and you hate Toledo, you don't have to take it to prove to anyone—including the boss who may be pressuring you to do so—that you're liberated. Being a happy person is what counts. If you know you can't be happy in Toledo, then a great job there won't make you happy.

And it does no good to listen to the testimonials of people who have sacrificed everything for their careers. They have paid a price. Take a look at their personal lives before using them as role models. A career isn't an end in itself. It is just one of the things that can enrich your life. And unless you want to be one-dimensional, you should strive to integrate your work into your personal life.

It's what's important to *you* that counts. Joyce recalls that when she was doing newspaper features, several editors told her that "real newspapering is covering hard news, city hall and fire stories." Just the thought of covering those kinds of stories filled her with boredom. She stayed with features and never let anyone talk her out of it.

Several years ago when she interviewed Mel Brooks about humor, she asked him how he wrote comedy. He said, "I know it works when I'm falling on the floor laughing as I'm writing it.

You can't write humor for anyone else—not even your brother Ernie. You've got to write it so it's funny to you."

If it's not what you want, pass it up! Women traditionally have had more of a problem sticking to what they want than have men, probably because we've been taught all our lives to be adaptable and accommodating. For many of us, a job offer is still a little like being asked to the prom. We are so happy that somebody wants us we forget what we want. Anyone who has ever endured a miserable prom date knows that saying yes just because she was asked is not the way to be happy.

Susan had a successful career going in retailing. She was a buyer for a major store chain that had recruited her and had her slated for a progression of bigger and better things. After two years as a buyer, Susan quit. Cold. Her friends, many of them fellow Harvard MBAs, couldn't believe it. She had been successful. She would be promoted. The company adored her. She was making a good salary and was about to make a lot more.

Susan told her friends she needed time to think about what she wanted to do. She had just passed thirty and didn't want to wake up one day to discover she had spent her life working at something she hated.

A month went by, with job offers coming in from other retailers hot on the trail of a woman MBA with experience in the field. Susan turned them all down, including store manager positions. Her friends passed from shock into dismay.

"I thought about it," she informed them, "and I've decided I don't like retailing. It's not the right field for me. I hate working six- and seven-day weeks, with no time to myself. I hate working holidays. And besides, I think the field is mostly mismanaged, and I have no patience for a lot of wasted time. And I feel a lot of my time was wasted."

She took three months to rest and think, then decided to return to school for her doctorate in business so that she could teach and write.

Perhaps, as you read her account, you think Susan is crazy. We think she's extremely sane. She decided retailing wasn't right for her, and that was that. And no one else's opinion carried as much weight as her own. She had also planned ahead enough to be financially able to afford a long vacation and return to school. Not only had she made a choice, but she took responsibility for her choice. If you are not happy at what you're doing, then the fact that your mother is proud of you or your friends envy you is simply not important.

This book begins with the woman on her own—and we are all on our own at the beginning of our career lives. Chapter by chapter, we move through the facets of our lives: men, friends, children, change, and a variety of other topics. When you read the book, don't skip over a section just because it doesn't immediately apply to you. There are underlying principles that carry over from one area to another.

Some of the principles we'll explain are Pay to Play, Shifting Gears, the Queen Bee Sydrome, and many more.

If we make you laugh or smile while reading this book, good. A sense of humor can often be a working woman's best friend. We've found you can laugh your way out of almost anything. Judy's story illustrates the point:

"The worst time I ever had was when I was eighteen and living in New York. I had taken an apartment with this wonderful gal, very sweet and charming. We shared a one-room-with-kitchen apartment that had belonged to her sister, who worked at *Vogue* and had painted the whole thing chocolate brown and black patent leather. It was at Ninety-Seventh Street and Fifth Avenue. It was overloaded with geriatrics. We didn't belong there. We were flower children to some extent.

"She had gone to Rome with her family, and I had just broken up with my first and longtime love, whom I had sent off to Oregon to pursue his academic career. I'm almost on the verge of suicide, and I tried to decide what's wrong. There was no light coming into the apartment.

"I decided I was going to save my life. Now how do I do that?

"The first thing that occurred to me was that the one way to save your life was to buy a TV, to have some noise in this apartment that had no light coming into it. I did, and all of a sudden all the things I had rejected in my childhood were coming back to me, or at least the TV was. It was one way of surviving. Then I called my friends, and things worked out great."

Mostly, this book is about sharing. We career women are every bit as brave and adventurous as our pioneer ancestors, and the help and support we can give each other can make the success any of us achieves only more rewarding.

TWO

ON
YOUR OWN

It wasn't until I moved out of my parents' house and into an apartment of my own that I ever experienced being alone with myself. Even in college I had a roommate and other girls in the dormitory for company. At first, living alone made me feel lonely. I seemed to have so many hours to fill after work. The first month was really strange; I felt so isolated. Then, little by little, I began to enjoy it. I bought a stereo and played all my favorite records. I read a lot, learned to cook, started playing the guitar again as I had in college. That all happened ten years ago. I'm married now, and my husband and I share many, many things. But I find I still need some time alone—to think, to sort things out—and I've built that into my marriage. Now being alone makes me feel like more of a person, not less.

I'm thirty-two and still single. I've lived alone for ten years, and although I know I'm one of those people who need a lot of time to themselves, I'd be kidding myself if I said I was never lonely. I have friends and hobbies and things I like to do, but there are times, like on a rainy Sunday, when everyone seems to be busy, that I feel lonely. I try to keep the loneliness to a minimum by scheduling my contact with people, but it does take planning. And if I have too much time alone, it depresses me. On the other hand, it depresses me if I have too little. I guess I see time alone as a positive and a negative. It's a positive because I need time to myself. It's a negative when I'm alone because I have no choice.

After marriage and the raising of two kids, time alone is my idea of dying and going to heaven. I never knew that silence—just plain quiet—could be so fulfilling. The kids are in school, and I work at home, so during the day I have the house to myself. I cherish that time not just because I can write without interruption, but because I can sit and think, savor memories of times with the family, sort myself out, see myself as a person, independent of being someone's wife and someone else's mother. And I find that by my having time alone, the quality of time I spend with my husband, my children, and my friends is so much better. I suppose that's because I now feel like a person with her own identity, not an appendage.

ESSENTIALLY ALL CAREER women start off on their own. They may move into an apartment and a new job right out of school, move out of their parents' home, or reenter the working world after years of child rearing. Later, throughout our careers, we all experience times when we have to stand up by, and for, ourselves, whether it's for an important decision in the office or for a unique piece of our personal lives.

While this chapter contains a lot of advice for single career women and those just starting out in new careers, it also lays the foundation for our discussions throughout the book. Learning to be your own person is the cornerstone of having it all, and what we have to say in this chapter is a big part of that.

We think everyone needs time alone. It gives you space to be yourself—breathing room in an often hectic, crowded life. As such, it's both a luxury and a necessity: a luxury because you can afford the time to be alone after organizing and gaining control of your life; a necessity because it gives you time for inner growth, for relaxation, and for reflection.

First Time Out

Being on your own for the first time—whether you're eighteen or forty—gives you the opportunity to form yourself as a human being, to broaden your knowledge, your interests, and your sense of the kind of life you want. You can observe people around you, choose what fits, and discard what doesn't. Best of all, you can prove to yourself that you can make it on your own.

In doing things for the first time, you may see yourself as a different person, someone who in many ways is a stranger to the old you. But as you become comfortable with being on your own, suddenly the pieces fit together, and the total effect is liberating.

There is a great advantage to starting out as a career woman. Choosing a career is different from just accepting a job. There are many working women in America, but only some of them are career women. When you choose a career, you plot a course for yourself, decide where you want to go and how you're going to get there. You plan for the experience you'll need, the credentials such as special or advanced degrees, and you plot the various options open to you for getting where you want to go. Your work efforts are *directed*, and you live not only for the present but for the future. It's important to keep in mind the distinction between a working woman and a career woman: A working woman will work for immediate goals; a career woman takes the long view and plans a life course.

When you begin as a career woman, you learn to live independently, learn to choose what you like in life and what you don't. You learn about the kind of living and working environment that suits you—you take an apartment on your own or share one; you enjoy a structured job or an unstructured one. You learn the kind of people you enjoy and those you can do without. You discover how you really like to spend your time. You learn how to entertain at home or find that you don't like to entertain and would rather go out. Of all the options available, you choose those that fit who you are, developing your own style and approach to your personal and professional life.

When Bettye came to New York, she came alone, college diploma in hand, with no job, no friends in the city, and no prospects that she knew of. What she did have was a sense of adventure and confidence in her ability to make things work somehow. She had saved enough money to stay at a hotel for women while she got to know the city and surveyed the job market. She gave herself one summer to succeed in New York.

No one told Bettye to come to New York. She just felt that nothing would ever happen in her life if she stayed in Texarkana. For her, New York represented the big world out there, and she wanted to succeed in it. She had enough confidence in her ability to cope on her own to come to a new city and make her way, to establish herself personally and professionally.

For both of us, those first few months of establishing ourselves as independent, both personally and professionally, were invaluable. Learning that you can cope, survive, and succeed is a terrific feeling—and it's something no one can give you but yourself.

By the end of the summer Bettye had landed her first job. After checking endless classified ads, visiting employment agencies and personnel departments, she accepted an entry-level job in the personnel field. More than her career had been launched. Her life as an independent· woman had begun.

Joyce came to New York at eighteen, a college dropout with one goal in mind: to become a working journalist. Although she had grown up in New Jersey, New York was as unfamiliar to her as if she had been brought up in Des Moines. She had never been on a subway, never been to an employment agency, never eaten alone in a coffee shop. She did her first day of job hunting in December, in the snow. On that first day she took her first subway ride, ate her first meal out alone, and made the rounds of the employment agencies. And she liked the feeling doing those things gave her—that she was on her own.

Every employment agency told Joyce the same thing: "You'll never get a job in journalism without a degree." But she was determined. Although she could have lived at home with her parents indefinitely, she wanted to strike out on her own, get that first job, become the journalist she had dreamed of being.

With incredible luck, on her second day she landed a job at the *Saturday Evening Post*. True, she was only a secretary, making the going rate of $85 a week. But she had gotten the first job, and she was at a well-respected magazine, where she could at least observe how professional journalism was done. And she was earning her way.

What Does It Cost to Be Single?

When you're single and live alone, there are two kinds of costs to consider—emotional and monetary.

Emotionally you'll have rough times living alone unless you develop a plan, a system for coping with being alone and for learning to enjoy it. Many of the single women we've interviewed have developed systems for making living alone as enjoyable as possible. When there is no single sustaining relationship in your life, you tend to spread out your need for companionship to family and friends. And you tend to plan ahead more and have contingency plans so that you don't spend more time alone than you want to.

"It takes more effort when you're alone," Susan says. "You really have to decide what you want to do and whom you want to do it with. In the end, I have one rule. If I can't find a willing companion to go to a movie or a museum or even take a vacation with, I'd rather go alone. That way I get to do what I want to do. But if I'm really needing companionship, then I'm willing to compromise on what we do. It's a trade-off."

You need to check inside yourself to see what your needs are and then to depend on yourself to fill them. Of course, friends and family will help, but only if you tell them what you need. One of the major benefits to be gained from living alone is learning what your emotional needs are and knowing that you're responsible for satisfying them.

Many women also find that they can satisfy many of their inner needs without turning to others. Just having time to think about their lives has made it easier for many women to cope. Being able to pursue hobbies and interests on their own schedule, in their own way, is also emotionally satisfying. Just creating an environment that suits *you*, from the color of the walls to the choice of furniture, can be tremendously satisfying if your surroundings reflect the inner you. There's time later for compromise and sharing. Time on your own is time to enjoy making unilateral decisions about your life and how you live it.

Dealing with the emotional cost of living alone is only solving half the problem. Money is a big issue. As inflation increases, the cost of living as a single escalates. How can you have the lifestyle you want with one paycheck?

You *have* to manage your money. Find the best possible apartment that you can afford. In some areas that will take a bigger chunk of your income than in others. In major urban areas like New York, housing is exery expensive. Plan for that.

Furniture costs money. And all household items, from sheets and towels to pots and pans, cost money. When you begin your life alone, it's best to have saved enough to cover initial expenditures for furniture and household goods.

Be selective. Not every piece you buy has to be an antique.

Nor do you have to plan to live with whatever you buy for a first apartment for the rest of your life. Figure out an overall budget for decorating. Then buy what you need and can afford. If you're handy, junk shops and the Salvation Army have older pieces that need repair or refinishing. If you can do it yourself, you save money and may even get better quality. Not everything has to be done at once. You may want to buy only major necessary items—a bed, a table, a couch or chair—at first. You can add more as you can afford it.

And before you decide what you can spend on your apartment, do an overall budget to see what you need for food, clothing, and other necessities. Then budget for entertainment, travel, any of the other things you want as part of your life.

Put your money where your interests are. If you really don't care about decorating, do the minimal amount you need to do to make your place habitable and forget it. If you really prefer jeans to designer clothes—and your job doesn't necessitate an extensive wardrobe—put less into clothes and more into what you want to spend your money on. The advantage in living alone is unlimited options. Use those options to determine what living alone will cost you—and what you can buy with your money.

Finding a Personal Style

The amount of time you need alone helps determine the kind of career you choose. And conversely, the kind of career you choose helps determine how much leisure time you need to spend alone. It's the chicken or the egg principle. For example, if you're in a people business, where the phone is constantly ringing and you're always on call, you may need more time alone to recharge batteries and just think. If you do a lot of solitary work—if you're in research or work at home—you may need less time alone during leisure hours. And if you know going in how much alone time you need, you may opt for the people job or the solitary one, depending on your needs.

As we see it, the world is divided up into four major types of people, in terms of time alone versus people contact. At one extreme is the Loner; at the other extreme is the People Person; in between are the Close but Not Too Close Person and the Nurturing Person. Without pigeonholing yourself, try to decide which type of person you are.

A Loner likes to spend most of her time alone. She generally does not like crowds or large parties and doesn't need intimate sharing on an ongoing basis. She has friends, but they needn't be crucial to her life. There may or may not be a special man in her life, and she may choose to stay single. In the end, she would rather commune with herself than with others.

She thinks nothing of taking a vacation by herself. In fact, often she prefers it because she can do what she wants to do when she wants to do it. She never expects people to drop everything to be with her if she needs company, nor does she like to be on call for others.

At the other extreme, the People Person not only loves people but needs them. She has a large circle of friends and acquaintances, likes to party or engage in other group activities, and often organizes these activities. She's a joiner and probably belongs to several organizations—and attends all the meetings. She likes sharing practically everything. She hates to be alone on a weekend and may even make backup plans in case her primary plans fall through. She knows at least several people just like her with whom she can fill several hours.

The Close but Not Too Close Person likes and needs people contact, but on a limited basis. She has good friends, but she needn't see them every day or even every week. She likes to schedule a good chunk of her time alone, and although she has friends, she reserves intimate sharing for a best friend or the man in her life, if there is one. She will choose to be alone when she needs to even if it means missing an activity with friends. If she's sharing her life with a man, he will know that she needs some time to herself and will give it to her; otherwise, she would feel "crowded" by him.

The Nurturing Person likes to give of herself, to share with friends and with the man in her life, if there is one. She has warm, close friends, not a crowd, but several individuals for intimate sharing. She prefers to spend her time with people she knows and cares about. Although she needs time alone, she will sometimes give it up to see someone she especially wants to spend time with. If there isn't a man in her life, one of her goals is to find the right one with whom to share her life. She enjoys giving—and getting—support.

It's important to know the kind of person you are before branching out into career and personal relationships. And choose without guilt. No one type is better than the other. Imagine being a Loner and choosing a career in public relations, where most of your days would be spent meeting and greeting people, charming them, wining and dining them. The rest of your days would be spent in meetings. Lots of people contact that would be bound to grate against the personality of a loner. Or imagine being a People Person and choosing a career in research, just you and your test tubes, with no one to talk to, relate to, or organize. It would be an alienating experience.

In the personal area, the same kinds of problems could arise. If you are a Nurturing Person and you decide to link up romantically with a Loner, the result could be disastrous. You would feel as if he weren't sharing himself with you. And he could very well feel as if you were suffocating him with your attention.

Once you've decided the kind of person you are, you can make logical career and lifestyle choices. You can feel perfectly at ease being a Loner, a People Person, a Close but Not Too Close Person, or a Nurturing Person. The only sin, if there is one, is not to know what kind of person you are, so that you find your personal life unsatisfactory without knowing why.

Making Time Alone Work for You

The women we interviewed are people who've established their careers and know pretty much who they are. Not surprisingly, they also know how to make time alone work for them.

Cathy, a divorced mother of two who organizes trade shows, spends her free time on a number of different interests. She has learned cabinetry and has built many pieces of her own furniture. She paints. She plays tennis and takes yoga classes. She has even learned transcendental meditation and gone through est and several other psychology courses. She says she likes to get underneath the surface of herself.

One son is grown and not living at home. The other is an active, creative teenager. She loves spending some of her free time with him and his friends, exchanging ideas and getting to know them as people. She gave her son a unique present, sending him to a self-actualization workshop which she had attended. He loved it, and they were able to share the experience.

She is approaching forty but looks like a woman in her twenties. Inside, she's ageless because she's constantly open to life and what it has to offer. Although she lives alone with her son, no one ever thinks of her as being lonely. And certainly no one would ever feel sorry for her because she has never felt sorry for herself. There's always something new and interesting in life for her to pursue. And she uses her free time to do as much of it as she can.

Karen is in her sixties, a writer and editor, the mother of three grown daughters, and the grandmother of three. Twice divorced, she's realized that she'd rather live alone. She has several passions in her life, writing being number one. She is working on her second novel. She is also an avid reader, loves the opera, loves to travel, enjoys art tremendously, and collects Impressionist paintings. Her apartment is filled with antiques she found by careful hunting in junk shops. With polishing and mending, she turns junk into treasures. She enjoys her daughters and her grandchildren, and she has many good friends. In terms of the things that really matter, she is one of the richest people we know. But she has chosen that richness in life. It didn't get there by accident.

It's important to make the decision to be alone, that you need time, whether it's ten minutes a day, or two days a week, just to indulge in your needs. People use their time alone for any number of different things. They read, they write, they paint, they garden, they do needlepoint, or they quilt. Sometimes they build their minds through techniques such as yoga and meditation. They may build their bodies with exercise classes or their own exercise routines, with tennis, golf, or any number of sports.

Some people find it necessary to take some time every day to be alone. Exercise can be perfect for this. We know one woman who just doesn't function well on her job if she hasn't run for an hour each morning. Walking to work instead of taking public transportation can be a way of getting exercise and being alone at the same time.

It should be noted that even if in normal times you are a People Person or a Nurturing Person, stress or strain can cause you to need more time alone than you usually do. You should be tuned into yourself enough to know when you need more time alone and should give that time to yourself.

Joyce has always needed time to be alone, to read, to write, to think, to play the piano, to listen to music. She has always had a people-oriented job, as a journalist and a public relations manager, so she plans at least several evenings a week of time alone and likes at least part of the weekend alone, even if it's just for a few hours.

"On weeks when I've overscheduled myself, I feel mentally exhausted," she says. "I just haven't had the time I need to recharge my batteries. And if I don't get that time, I tend to lose my sense of perspective. I make time for myself, and I enjoy it. You get a sense of yourself from being alone that you just can't get from anything else. Once I've had that time alone, I'm the most nurturing person I know. But I have to have it both ways."

Are You Making the Best of Your Time Alone?

This checklist is designed to help you evaluate how you're using your time alone. Is it wasted or productive? Is it enjoyable or boring? Is it a plus, a minus, or just a zero? Since time alone is a part of your life, you should use it to its full advantage.

1. Do you schedule time alone for yourself?
2. Do you plan and manage your time alone as effectively as you do time spent with others?
3. Are there hobbies and interests you like to pursue on your own?
4. Would you plan activities on your own—see a movie, visit a museum, take a vacation?
5. When you see someone else doing any of these things alone, how do you feel about that person?
6. Do you look forward to time alone? Do you dread it? Do you just not think about it?
7. How comfortable are you about telling friends you've spent time alone?
8. Do you like to accomplish things when you're alone, or would you rather just relax and curl up with a good book?
9. Do you feel more in touch with yourself when you're alone?
10. At the end of a day alone, how do you usually feel? Refreshed? Relaxed? Anxious? Lonely? Depressed?

When You're Forced into Being Alone

So far we've discussed the joys of solitude in terms of choosing to be alone or have time alone. But sometimes it's not our choice to be alone. Through death, divorce, the breakup of a relationship, relocation to a new city, we find ourselves alone. And that can be traumatic or even tragic.

When someone you love dies, it is a devastating loss. There is no easy way to cope, no glib answer to the pain you feel.

Maria had just begun her own business when her husband died. She was numb, in shock, even though he had been very ill for several months.

"If I hadn't had my daughter and the business, I don't know what I would have done," she says today. "Steve was so much a part of my life. I loved him so much. Just recently I cleaned out the attic and found a lot of his business papers. I sat there and cried. It was like losing him all over again.

"What do you do? You just go on. That's what I did. I know

that Steve would have wanted me to. And I had no choice. I had to support myself and my twelve-year-old daughter.

"In a way, I died myself. It's been five years now, and it's been a slow process of coming fully back to life."

For a widow, the sense of loss goes through cycles: the initial shock and numbness, the first year of major readjustment, and then the constant feeling of loss that usually becomes less intense but is still felt. When you lose someone you love, time does help heal the wound, but it's a wound that heals in stages.

Women who have been divorced know a different kind of loss. We both have been through it and agree that even when you know that it was a bad marriage and that getting a divorce is the right decision, it is a wrenching, traumatic process which can leave you feeling—at least for a while—like a displaced person.

When Joyce was first divorced, she suddenly became conscious of couples. The whole world seemed to be coupled. She felt she was the only single person alive. She had married when she was twenty and divorced at twenty-two. She had been brought up to believe that marriage was forever. Hers had lasted only two years.

What do you do? You cope. You get a little help from your friends. You rebuild your life, try to focus on the positive aspects of your situation, but also acknowledge the negative, painful ones. It's okay to cry. It even makes you feel better. Talking to other women—and men—who have been through it can help ease the pain. At least it lets you know that others have been there before you.

Sometimes just redoing your physical environment can help. Build a nest of one. If you have good, quality friends, they'll be there for you. If you have the love and support of your family, that helps enormously. And of course, the sheer passage of time helps. You begin to feel better.

If you have lived on your own before marriage, coping with divorce will probably be easier. If you haven't lived alone before, try to treat it as an adventure.

Sometimes, when people are forced into being alone, depression and anxiety can become major problems to deal with. It's important to figure out what's making you anxious or depressed and to sort through the problem. Get help if you need it, from a friend or a professional in the area of your need.

When Joyce was first divorced, she found herself afraid to be alone. On the surface, it was fear for her physical safety. Someone would break into her apartment and attack her. Each night, before going to bed, she would check all the doors and windows, making sure they were locked. For several weeks she didn't sleep very well, convinced that there was some threat to her safety. She wasn't normally an anxious or apprehensive person, so she knew there was some underlying problem that was making her afraid. A friend really triggered the solution when he said, "You know, being alone is not being unloved."

He had put his finger on her real fear: that she would be alone for the rest of her life. Joyce knew, intellectually, this wasn't the case, that she had warm and loving friends and that she would probably fall in love again. Once she knew what her hidden fear was, the fear for her physical safety disappeared.

If traumatic things are happening in your life and your behavior becomes odd or unusual for you, try to figure out the underlying problem. Talk with friends, family, a minister, or a counselor. Seek some kind of help. There's nothing weak about needing and seeking support to help get you through a trying time.

Rebecca has an excellent way of looking at this issue. Happily enjoying her second marriage, she recalls the bleak days after her divorce, when she had her daughter to rear and was learning to earn her own living. "In retrospect, it was a tempering experience," she says. "Life tempers you by what you go through. If you learn from experiences—even negative experiences—you emerge stronger, in the same way steel is tempered by heat. What you thought you couldn't survive, you find you can."

If you're alone because you've relocated, the best way to ease the loneliness is to immerse yourself in your new community. Take courses. If you're a joiner, look for clubs or organizations that might interest you. Check newspaper columns and listen to local radio and TV stations for activities in your area that you might enjoy. Take up a new sport or hobby. Learn tennis or bridge. Once you meet one or two people, they'll introduce you to others. It takes a little time, but it happens if you let it.

Designing a Life System

Having it all means having a game plan. And perhaps nothing takes more organization than living on your own and succeeding at it. You have to be all things for yourself. Or you have to develop systems to free your time. The routine chores of life have to be accomplished: You need to eat, to have clean clothes to wear, to have a clean place to live, to maintain your looks and your health, and somehow to make it all enjoyable.

If you can afford it, we advocate letting services help you as much as possible. And double-check your budget before deciding that you can't afford to have someone else worry about some of your routine chores. For example, if you live in an apartment, you'd have to do laundry in a pay machine. Compute the cost of the machine and what your time is worth; then balance it against sending your laundry out. A cleaning woman can be seen as a luxury, but for some people it's a necessity. If you have a busy work and social schedule and like to entertain at home a lot, you may need to have a cleaning woman or service. Check friends for references, and shop around for prices and what you can expect.

Judy has never had a cleaning woman and doesn't view cleaning the two-bedroom apartment she shares with her husband as a chore. "I designed everything for easy maintenance. A lot of Lucite and plastic that can be wiped clean. Virtually no glass or wood to be polished. I invested in a terrific vacuum cleaner that picks up quickly and efficiently. I can do a thorough cleaning in two hours. And my husband helps."

Whichever route you choose, make sure it's making the best use of your time, energy, and money.

If you cook for yourself, choose foods that are easy to prepare or that can be prepared in advance and heated. Several women we talked to make casseroles or other dishes they can freeze and defrost as needed.

Organization can really help. Make a list of your weekly chores, and estimate the time it takes you to do them. Consider all the options. Is it faster, cheaper, and easier to order all your meat monthly from a butcher than to buy it on a weekly or daily basis? If you live in an urban area, is it really easier in the long run to have groceries, laundry, and cleaning delivered than it is to make several trips to pick them up? In many cities, supermarkets will deliver groceries at no extra charge. The only additional cost is a tip to the delivery boy.

Diet, Health, Beauty, and Fashion

Some people feel that if they're not cooking for someone else, what they eat doesn't matter. That's nonsense. There has been enough written on nutrition and health to set the record straight on that score. You owe it to yourself to eat right, especially if you are a woman who works and plays hard. You need a balanced diet of foods with high nutritional value. Lack of time is not an excuse. You can put together a salad in minutes. You can broil or sauté chicken, steak, fish, lamb, or veal in minutes. If you can only boil water and open a can, use the water to boil eggs and make the can tuna fish. You might add some cottage cheese and a salad of mixed greens and vegetables, and you've just served dinner.

It's easy to say you don't have time for your health, but you need to make the time. Regular medical checkups are important. Your doctor can tell you what your system needs. He may recommend a multiple vitamin to supplement your diet if you're not eating properly, or he may give you a diet to follow.

Bettye has always believed that success begins with good health. If you don't have it and maintain it, you're not going to be able to do all the things you want.

Take time to be good to yourself and take care of yourself. Aside from eating right, you should take the time you need to sleep and relax. A doctor friend of Joyce's used to recommend the Weekend Rest Cure. Go away for the weekend; relax; get away from it all. If you can't go away, act as if you're away. Make no plans. Take the phone off the hook. Then do whatever you please. It works and can have a marvelous restorative effect.

As John Molloy and a legion of others have told us, part of being successful in the business world is looking good. All you need is a plan for beauty maintenance and a little fashion sense.

Many women make the mistake of beginning their beauty regimen with makeup. Wrong. First, you maintain the skin. Clean, glowing, healthy skin is the key. And with the variety of good products on the market today, it needn't take a lot of time, but you must have a routine. Determine your skin type—is it dry, normal, a combination of dry and oily, or oily? Then choose the right products for your skin. For your face, you need a cleanser—either liquid or a bar of some sort. You should condition your skin with a toner, right after washing. And you should use a moisturizer under makeup or without makeup. If your skin needs a deep cleaning—if you have blemishes or blackheads or you just want to slough away dead surface skin—you can do it yourself with a mask, or you can treat yourself to a professional facial. If you've never had one, you owe it to yourself to try it. Not only does your skin look and feel better, but you get to feel totally pampered while someone else worries about taking care of you. In most cities, a facial can be had for under $50. You'll still want to buy a mask for at-home maintenance, especially if you live in an urban area where pollution can adversely affect your skin.

You can pamper your body as well as your face in a variety of ways. If you like baths, try a bubble bath or a mineral bath which can help soothe aching muscles. Bath oils can make skin smooth and prevent drying, especially in colder weather. A good hand- and body-moisturizing cream or lotion is essential. It's a good idea to keep hand cream at the office, especially if you work with paper and ink a lot because they can be drying.

In terms of grooming, the second most important person in your life is your hairdresser. You need someone who knows and cares about you and your lifestyle, who can help you choose a flattering hairstyle that's easy to cope with on your own. There are women who enjoy going to the hairdresser once or twice a week, but if you're like many career women, you simply don't have time for that, so you need a hairstyle you can do yourself and quickly.

Your hairdresser will know when and how to condition your hair. If you color, streak, or frost your hair, he will know how to do it expertly to create a natural effect. Ask him to recommend a shampoo and conditioner you can use at home, in between visits.

Hands and feet shouldn't be ignored. Well-manicured nails are attractive and valuable. Hands are wonderful for gesturing with, getting a point across with, and there's something very esthetically appealing, to men and women, about well-manicured nails on well-cared-for hands. You can use a colored polish or a clear one, or you can simply buff your nails to shine naturally, but you can't ignore them. Even if you don't notice them, others will.

Feet can be pampered in any number of ways. There's even a new appliance that will soak and massage tired feet. You can do your own pedicure or treat yourself to one. You must have shoes that fit and are comfortable. Invest in good shoes that are stylish but have lots of support. If you're on the go all the time, feet can really take a beating. And no one is at her best when her feet hurt.

Makeup is back in vogue, and it's a tool to be used, like any other. It can accentuate your looks and make you more attractive. Choose a makeup that suits your style. Examine fashion and beauty magazines for ideas and experiment. Many cosmetics counters have skilled makeup artists who will do your makeup for you and advise you on what to use and how to use it. You don't want to look garish, and you don't want to look like a plain Jane. You want to appear attractive, so choose accordingly.

Apply Time Management Principles to Beauty Routine

There have been enough books and seminars on how time management techniques help you control your business day, but no one has applied these techniques to women's out-of-the-office routines. If you think about it, time out of the office is just as valuable as—if not more so than—time in the office, so it makes sense to manage it so that the routine is out of the way as quickly as possible.

When you choose a beauty regimen, keep time management in mind. You need to organize your routine for optimum efficiency. You need to plan to the minute how long it takes you to get totally groomed and dressed in the morning. Hairstyles can be chosen for how much time you want to spend on them. So can makeup and skin cleansing routines.

Strive to do two things at once. We've discovered you can polish your nails and blow dry your hair at the same time. Once your nails are polished, you can safely handle the dryer, allowing them to dry without smearing. You can also have part of your breakfast while doing your grooming routine, if you can bear to eat standing up. Orange juice or a nutritious protein drink can be drunk while you're applying your makeup or doing your hair. The possibilities are endless for combining two or three routine chores into one time frame.

Time management and grooming extend to the office. You may be a busy executive, but you're also a person who wants to be able to look her best all day—even on short notice or when the unexpected happens.

If you have business dinners or meetings in the evening or go directly from work to an outside engagement, you may want to keep beauty supplies at the office for a quick touch-up at the end of the day. Leading a busy life takes planning, and you want to look your best on a busy schedule, so it makes sense to plan ahead with the necessary supplies.

Keep at the office a duplicate set of makeup, a nail file, a bottle of nail polish and some remover, tissues and cotton balls, for applying and removing makeup and polish, a bottle of your favorite fragrance, and some other helpful items, like an extra pair of stockings in case you develop a midday run, a sewing kit for minor repairs—a torn hem or missing button—hand cream, and a toothbrush and toothpaste. You can store them all unobtrusively in a desk drawer.

These tips may seem minor, but they're all a part of time management techniques for the woman who is more than her career. Once you organize all this routine into systems, you don't have to think about it; everything just falls into place. It may look effortless to those observing you, but as with most things in life, what looks effortless takes time and planning.

Now that your body is accounted for, what do you put on it? For women who don't work, shopping can be a pastime, a fun activity. For most working women, especially those with heavily scheduled lives, shopping is a problem. There simply isn't the time to browse at will. But a career woman needs clothes—enough of them and ones that work for her lifestyle—more than anyone. What's the solution?

Planning. We shop by the season. And we make a list of what we have before we add anything. We look at styles and colors. We check whether something we've had for a year or two can be adapted by a clever tailor to fit the latest look. We check colors because what makes a wardrobe work is that pieces go with other pieces. Building around neutrals is really helpful. If you start with a black, beige, brown, gray, or navy blue palette, you can add color in shirts and accessories without totally redoing your wardrobe.

After we survey what we have, we make a list of what we need. Reading fashion magazines helps you see what the trends are. The trick is to fit the trends to your lifestyle. Simple classics work best in business and are better investments because you can wear them longer. Anything too costumey or outlandish is distracting in business and looks dated very fast.

After we make a list of what we need, we estimate a realistic price for each item and compare it to the budget we've established for the season. If the cost is higher than our budget, we check to see whether we can afford to spend more, or we cut back on what we need.

We go shopping only after we've established a budget and a list. We usually plan one or two days, generally on the weekend, for our shopping expeditions. We have several retail and discount stores we use regularly. We look for quality clothes that can mix. We check workmanship—if it's not made well, it won't last. We look at how the garment is finished, at the seams, the hem, the detailing. We check the fabric content. Is it washable? Does it need to be dry cleaned? Does it wrinkle easily? Can stains be removed easily? If it wrinkles easily, it's not a wonderful work garment. As you sit and stand, you get wrinkles in the garment. By the end of the day you can look a mess.

Susan told us she always buys several knit outfits—a dress, a jacket and skirt because "when everything else really needs to go to the cleaner's, I can always get by with a knit." The wear and tear on a good knit are better than on most popular fabrics.

You should have enough clothes so that something is always ready to go. If your separates mix well, you can create your own outfits, for variety and flexibility.

We avoid impulse buying. Usually what you buy on impulse is a mistake, and mistakes sit in the closet. Impulse buying can also wreck your budget and keep you from buying what you really need and want. It takes self-discipline, but it works.

You can save a lot of money by buying clothes at a discount if you know what you're buying. If you don't, enlist a friend who does to come with you or stick to retail establishments you trust.

Many department stores have personal shoppers who will help you put a wardrobe together. As they get to know you, they will select things with you in mind, and you can choose an entire wardrobe in a couple of hours. You will pay retail prices for this service, but if you can afford it, it's worth the money. Or you might use the service once or twice to learn how to put things together if you need some expertise.

Two other essentials are a good cleaner and a good tailor. Many garments will need alterations, from the hem to the length of the sleeves. You need someone who does expert tailoring in a minimum amount of time at reasonable prices. Shop around. Ask friends. A good tailor is invaluable. So is a good cleaner. If clothes are an investment, he can help them look their best. Again, ask around.

You need someone who presses beautifully, can take proper care of fine or fragile fabrics, can remove spots and stains, can store clothes from one season to the next, and can make minor repairs if you don't have the time or the inclination.

Another service you need is a good shoe repair place. Heels run down quickly. Shoes get scuffed and scraped. Boots need refurbishing or treating for bad weather. You don't want to look "down at the heels."

I Am *Not* My Job!

Once you have the details of life under control, the rest of the time is for your pleasure and enjoyment. Your leisure time is crucially important to your well-being. It's the time to nurture yourself, pleasure yourself, create new challenges for yourself. It's the time for personal growth. If you think you don't have time for yourself, think again. We've formulated a key principle, really the principle underlying this book: I AM *NOT* MY JOB!

It may sound self-evident, but in practice, for many people, it isn't. If your idea of a great weekend is going into the office to get caught up, if quiet evenings at home mean reading professional literature or gossiping with co-workers about office politics, then you've missed the point of leisure time. And you've missed the point of work. Work is only a part of our lives—an important part, but one that can be self-destructive if we try to make it a substitute for a complete life.

Being alone provides a wonderful opportunity to discover your personal dimensions, to explore your values, find out what's really important to you. It's a good time for dreaming the big dreams: the kind of life you want; the kind of man you want; the kind of people and things you enjoy; the kind of career you want. It's a time to learn new hobbies or pursue new interests or get involved in ongoing pursuits.

When Susan was alone in Detroit, knowing no one, she bought and refinished furniture, made curtains and pillows, totally decorated a two-bedroom apartment. She managed to use her alone time profitably, and she got to keep the positive residual effects—beautifully refinished furniture to enjoy.

Whether you pursue one hobby or several, whether you're an indoor or an outdoor person, time alone can be valuably and enjoyably used. And the self-knowledge you gain can be tremendously helpful in future decisions you make about your life.

You can explore your own femininity: What does it mean to you to be a woman today? What is feminine? What is masculine? Your sexual identity is part of your overall identity as a person. With women's roles changing so quickly, it's important to define for ourselves who we are, what we expect, what we want to achieve and accomplish.

The Virtues of Solitude

If time alone is used well, we come away knowing ourselves better, feeling at ease and at peace with ourselves. And from that base of inner harmony, we can build rewarding relationships, one independent human being to another. Once we know what we want, what we like, what we prefer, we can choose friends and lovers who suit us, complement us, nurture and support us. We can choose careers and interests that challenge us, broaden us, increase our awareness.

If we feel successful on the inside, if we are content with ourselves, then we'll attract people like us. And we'll be real—not our mothers, not an assertiveness-training stereotype or a TM groupie, but a whole, thinking person who has acquired values by choice and has established an identity as a mature human being.

In order to reach that stage, we need to take care of ourselves and see it as a legitimate concern, not a selfish whim on our part. It's a necessity to maintain our physical and mental health, to make our free time work for us, whether we want to be alone or to reach out to friends and loved ones. The essence of being an assertive, independent woman is to know your own needs and take care of them. If your own needs aren't taken care of, how can you possibly take care of anyone else's, from your husband to your child, your friend, your employer?

Central to taking care of yourself is knowing what exactly is bothering you at any given time you're feeling stress. So many people will say, "I'm having a bad day," without analyzing *what* is bad. Others will say they hate their jobs, without identifying what they hate—the people, the hours, the detail, whatever it is. Escape—physical or mental—isn't the answer. If you leave a job you hate without knowing why you hated it, you may find yourself hating the next job just as much. If you "escape" through drink or drugs, not only will you not solve your current problem, but you'll find yourself with bigger ones to deal with. A little self-knowledge goes a long way.

It will give you a sense of having control of your life, and that brings with it a feeling of confidence and competence: confidence in your ability to cope with all life has to offer and competence to achieve success in whatever you choose.

You can store up moments of self-knowledge and self-acceptance that can sustain you for the rest of your life. At rock bottom, deep down where you live, you know who you are, and you're willing to share who you are with those you choose.

Now you're ready to branch out.

THREE

THE
JOYS OF
FRIENDSHIP

My friends mean more to me than my immediate family. That family was never there for me when I was growing up. As I've grown, my standards for friendship have changed. When I was in my twenties, I equated having a lot of friends with being popular. If I was invited to all the right parties, that was terribly important to me. It's not anymore. I don't need a lot of friends. I need—and have—a few people I trust to tell me the truth. They are also people who are all terribly funny. They share my humor and wit, but more than that, they share my zest for life. All my friends want it all.

I have very good friends: people whom, if I need them, I know

I can call. I can depend on them if I need someone to talk to. Age has nothing to do with it. It's a chemistry, a feeling that the same basic things are important to you. And when you have people like that for friends, it is the most marvelous thing.

My friends are like me, busy, involved, lots of things happening in their lives at the same time. For one reason or another, we can go weeks, sometimes even months without seeing each other, but the bond is always just as strong. We've been thinking about each other. My friendships have a continuity which has nothing to do with calling each other every day. When I need a friend or want to touch base, I pick up the phone, and we can talk for a couple of hours or we'll get together and stay up all night talking. I'm always there for my friends when they need me, and they're always there for me. They fill my life with caring.

As IMPORTANT AS friendships are to people in general, they are doubly important to career women. We're out there, often in uncharted territory, doing things for the first time, learning to cope with multifaceted lives, expanding our professional horizons, and all these challenges take a lot of nurturing. As we learned in Chapter Two, nurturing begins at home when we learn to stand on our own and draw on our inner strength. But nobody makes it alone. Friends form a nurturing core, a communications network, a counseling service, a reference point.

In this chapter we're going to talk about all the values career women can derive from friendships. We'll examine the Old Girls' Network and why it's important for women to form one and plug into it on a consistent basis. We'll talk about business friends and personal friends and how they often overlap in the life of a career woman. We'll talk about giving and getting support, how to cheer each other on in our triumphs and shore each other up in our defeats. We'll also hit on the pitfalls of women-to-women friendships—the negatives to avoid so that they don't drain your positive energy. We'll talk about your changing status as you move up the business ladder and how that affects friendships—how to maintain friendships with those who really have important values in common with you, how to let go of the more superficial relationships as circumstances change.

If you started your career on a clerical or secretarial level—and many of us have—you may find, as you move up, that work friends you made as a secretary may not remain friends if they stand still in their careers and you move on. And the reason won't necessarily be envy, but just a change in interests and emphasis. On the lower levels of the corporate structure, people put in their nine-to-five days and look forward to going home. They are not necessarily absorbed in what they do although they may enjoy their jobs while they're there. If you move beyond that level and begin having increased responsibility and pay, your work may become more a part of your life and will absorb you more. You may want friends with whom you can discuss business strategy or management problems. The friends from your secretarial days may want to discuss their latest vacations or their new houses. If you have interests other than work in common with them, the friendship can survive and even flourish. But if work was the primary thing you had in common, the friendship will fade away.

Remember the I Am Not My Job Principle from Chapter Two. Work isn't the only thing to have in common with friends; basic values in lots of areas pull you together. So long as those remain intact, friendships can survive even if you become chairwoman of the board and your friend is still a secretary.

A significant part of having it all is filling your life with positive, nurturing people. Whether or not you have a man in your life, whether or not you have a family, friends can enrich your life in lots of ways, big and small. As an active woman with a full-time career you will find it increasingly necessary to choose quality over quantity in friendships, to find those people you most want to share your life with, to pursue them, and to maintain these friendships.

Choosing Woman-to-Woman Friendships

The best thing about being career women today is that we have virtually unlimited alternatives. We are truly in the options market, and friendship is one area where choosing the right options can bring us tremendous dividends. Forming friendships with other career women makes sense: We have a major element of our lives in common—our careers. But as big a factor as a career is, it isn't the only criterion for choosing friends. Since your time and energy are limited, you will want to choose those women who have the most in common with you, whose company you most enjoy on a consistent basis, whose values and goals you understand and share.

Because career women are independent and self-motivated, we have become the primary source of support for one another, as opposed to the precareer days, when women couldn't stand alone and therefore didn't have unlimited choices. We can now meet and choose each other, independent of the interests of our families or even our husbands. That's a crucial difference because it means we can choose people who reflect our interests and values, thus reinforcing our own sense of self through our friendships. Also, because we have control of our lives through setting and achieving our own goals and earning our own livings, we have a positive frame of reference for friendships. The focus is on ourselves as doers—sharing values, information, and support with other doers.

Dealing Through Strength

If you deal through strength in your own life and in relationships with others, you'll find you'll have higher expectations for yourself and be able to meet them. If you let others know you expect them to be able to cope, they may surprise you—and themselves. Everybody wins, and nobody loses.

When you form friendships based on mutual strength, the relationships become positive reinforcements of your ability to make your own life, to have all the things you want. The friendships encourage positive emotions—admiration, respect, trust, and love. Even problems are seen in perspective; even when things go wrong, you are ultimately in control of your own life, and it will all work out. And you see your friends that way—as people who are winners, not losers, so that even if something bad happens to them, you know they'll survive, cope, and ultimately win. All of us who have made the decision to pursue careers, to be independent, have worked to develop our own strength. It's a value and a virtue to take pride in.

Never let your strength be used against you by someone who presents herself as weak. As women have gained increasing control of their lives, some have found friends, acquaintances, and even family members only too willing to cash in on their strength by saying something like "It's so easy for you and so hard for me. I don't know how you do it, but you just breeze through life and never have any problems." People who use that are playing on guilt. They make you feel as if, through chance or blind luck or divine intervention, you go through life like Wonder Woman, as if there's no problem you can't solve, and that's just the way your life is. There is no acknowledgment of the time, effort, and sometimes the pain of what you've gone through in your own life in order to reach the point where you're fully in control. From the premise that you have been mysteriously blessed with strength through no effort of your own, they proceed to how you *owe* them your help because you are strong and they are weak. Guilt rears its ugly head.

How do you cope? You refuse to play that game. If you've earned your own independence and whatever happiness you have in your life, you are entitled to enjoy it without guilt. People who want to manipulate you through guilt are not really caring friends, and you needn't worry about naming the issue to them, gently but firmly. Once they know they can't manipulate your strength, they'll have to deal through strength themselves in order to get the benefit of your support and counsel.

Think about it. The people you really respect and care about are ones you know will survive, will cope, with or without you. You want to help them because you care about them, but you know that primarily they will want to do it on their own and that they'll accept your help only when they know they have to do so in order to clear up the temporary chaos. At base, that's a virtue you love and respect in yourself: the ability to cope with life on your own terms. Don't accept less from your friends. They'll love you for your standards and implied good judgment of them. If you treat people like basket cases, they'll act like them.

If you've always had unlimited time to listen to your friends and have suddenly begun a new career or job, started writing a book, had a child, or gotten married, you need to let friends know that your situation has changed and your once-unlimited time now has limits. Good friends will understand and will be supportive of you by not making unfair demands on your time.

When Karen was writing her first book, she knew her leisure time was going to be severely limited. She simply announced to friends that she would not be available to socialize until after the book was written (she was writing while pursuing a full-time career as a journalist). If she found herself with an unexpected few hours of leisure time because she was working ahead of her deadline, she could call a friend and say, "I have some time. Are you free?" She understood perfectly if her friend wasn't, and her good friends were usually so delighted to be able to see her that they'd make the time when she had some.

Friends as a Support System

What we as career women need to remember is that the greatest help, the greatest source of strength we have, is each other. When we began discussing this book, we knew who our best sources of information would be—not career counselors or psychiatrists or poll takers or "experts," but other career women. We knew we could learn from their experiences and pass these experiences on to you.

Day to day, life operates in much the same way. As career women we have certain things in common. We work at something we enjoy, and that absorbs us. We have long-term goals and a plan to achieve them. We have lots of energy and are willing to expend it to succeed. We all are learning as we go along, having lots of "first" experiences. We are independent and try our best to cope. When we exchange our ideas and feelings, our experiences and our viewpoints, we support each other. We see our friends as a support system. And you should, too.

Examples make it easier to understand. You get a promotion, and you want to tell someone. You pick up the phone and call a friend. She shares your delight, and she knows what you're feeling; she's been there. Or, as happened to Bettye when she found she was pregnant, she called the women she knew who had worked while pregnant to get their advice on the best way to handle her pregnancy and her career at the same time. When Joyce relocated to Ohio, she called one of her best friends who had relocated several times to get pointers on everything from what her new employer should provide in terms of expenses to how to meet people in her new city. And her friend prepared Joyce for some of the feelings of loneliness and disorientation she herself had experienced.

You share common experiences with each other, nurture and applaud each other. It's a give-and-take kind of relationship. Reciprocity is key to building supportive friendships. You should strive to be a trader of values, trading yours with those of your friends. If you're a giver or a taker, but not both, you won't be very successful at building support systems.

For most women, as they branch out in their careers and in their lives, their friendships grow, diversify, and prosper. Most of the women we interviewed had formed friendships in a variety of ways and through a variety of circumstances. Judging from our own experiences, that's the way it happens.

In thinking about how support systems develop, Joyce reflected on her own friendships and saw how varied they are. One friend is from childhood. Although they've been separated geographically for long periods of time, their friendship remains as strong as it was when they saw each other every day, put out the school newspaper together, and compared notes on dates. Another friend was a co-worker who became her assistant and later replaced her in Westchester. Although there are vast differences in their backgrounds, experiences, and ages, the tie between them is very strong, even though the tie of a common workplace hasn't existed for two years. Through this friend, Joyce made another friend, the vice-president of a major jewelry firm. They became fast friends as well. She made another friend while doing a story on a woman who had opened her own business in Westchester. After the interview they both knew they would become and remain friends. Four years later that's still the case. In Akron there were several co-workers and staff members who became and remain close, as well as several women Joyce met covering the community and a free-lance writer who wrote pieces for the lifestyles section.

Bettye has made friends in much the same way. She has three close friends from her college days. They live far apart geographically but manage to stay in touch with phone calls and visits. Another friend is an executive recruiter she works with in business and has become close to. Another is a co-worker. Still others remain from her banking days. And another is a friend of a friend whom Bettye called for advice on her pregnancy. That initial phone call led to friendship.

Susan plugs into her fellow Harvard MBAs—men and women—when she's having a work problem or needs to make a career decision. "We have the same frame of reference," she says. Because Susan has had several years' experience in fashion retailing, some of the women from her MBA class ask her advice on their wardrobes. She will even go on shopping trips with them, as a consultant. "In a way, we trade on each other's strengths," she says. "We each have our areas of expertise, and we share information. It's all on an informal basis, but it works."

Although Susan includes her fellow Harvard MBAs in her support system, it's wider than that. She has two friends from childhood she still sees, several friends from her undergraduate days she still visits with, and friends from the various places she's worked over a ten-year period.

The examples are endless. But if the support system is really working, then it feeds itself, with one friend introducing another to still more people, on the basis of common interests and goals. These friends are supportive on an *ongoing* basis, and it's part of every career woman's security blanket to know that she has a little help from her friends.

Forming the Old Girls' Network

Men have had an Old Boys' Network for years. It's a club with no formal charter, no scheduled meetings, no duly elected officers. Nevertheless, it's a network that exists and, on an informal but effective basis, has helped men in their careers. Men come to forming a network quite naturally. It is really an easy transition from team sports or teamwork to having a network of business associates.

Women are just learning to form networks, but we feel it's very important. A large part of building a successful career is being in the right place at the right time, knowing what opportunities are available, and having entrée to the people who decide who gets the jobs. Men have known this for years and have communicated this information to each other. Women are just beginning to do the same.

One element of forming a network is getting to know people in your company and in your field. Professional organizations and clubs are often helpful. Annual conventions and meetings are good places to form and plug into a network. Women in the same field can make each other aware of positions and opportunities, tell them the best way to approach a new job, how to package themselves.

For many women who have risen through the corporate ranks, their mentors have been men who have helped them along at each step and given counsel and advice, training, and further education when necessary. Men are still doing this for women, and if a network of both sexes is forming, all the better.

In the meantime, many women are now in at least middle-management positions in which they can help and counsel women who are coming up in the ranks. Sadly, for some women who were exceptions in the corporate world of men, once they reached positions of power, they wanted to have a monopoly on them and worked actively to keep other women down. We call this the Queen Bee Syndrome, and there's nothing more destructive or demoralizing for a fledgling career women to encounter than a Queen Bee in her prime.

Her motivation goes like this: She worked and clawed her way up from the secretarial pool. She had to work at least twice as hard as the men around her, twice as many hours for twice as many years to get where she is. No one helped her (at least so she thinks). She's always felt that building her career was a battle—she wanted in, and others wanted to keep her out. Because the trappings of power were so long in coming, she's determined to hold onto them. No one—man or especially younger woman—is going to come along and even share her power, let alone usurp it. In order to ensure her position, she makes certain that those who work for her never—or rarely—come in contact with upper management. She gives out titles and raises only grudgingly. She must have final say on everything herself and, of course, takes final credit. If someone who works for her has a suggestion of a better, faster, or cheaper way to get the job done, she is instantly suspicious that the person is after her job. Good or bad, the suggestion dies aborning. She'd rather continue doing things her way than delegate.

No one ever moves from her department into another department within the company. And no one gets promoted from within, or if he or she does, it's only a half step. She deeply resents the younger women coming along who don't seem to share the fear that has always been part of her mental set. These young women actually feel as if they will be able to succeed, and after the war she's been through, she doesn't think anyone who comes after her should have it any easier.

Of course, this is a person essentially to be pitied because her self-confidence is at zero level. How she could have become so insecure is even understandable. But the main point to remember is that she's trouble, and if you can, avoid her. Even a job with a great salary and great title will bring you nothing but grief if you work for a Queen Bee. She will share nothing with you. You will never get the full picture or make any policy decisions. You will be one of her minions. Whether she comes across as mommy or the Wicked Witch of the West, there's no mistaking her message—you are the underlings, and she is the boss.

A valuable lesson can be learned from the Queen Bee: Never become one. It will diminish you as a person because it's destructive behavior. It will diminish your effectiveness in your company because everyone will know exactly what you're doing and will have contempt for you for doing it. If you're secure in your own abilities, it's a pleasure to help those who work for you succeed. And their success will guarantee your success. Teamwork is an essential part of functioning in the corporate world. If you learn effective management techniques, including how to develop staff and how to delegate responsibility, you will become even better at your job. There's a particular joy that comes from seeing someone you've developed move out on his or her own. We've both had this experience, and so have many of the women we interviewed. You're spreading the wealth, sharing your experience, and helping clear the path for other women and men.

When Sandra needed an assistant in her recruiting business, she had to look no farther than her talented secretary, who had learned the ropes from the inside out. Now her secretary—we'll call her Pat—has become a full-fledged executive recruiter under Sandra's tutelage.

When Joyce left Westchester, her assistant was promoted into her job. And when she got the job, she knew exactly how to function in it because she had been exposed to all aspects of how the thirty-person department was run.

As we learn to deal through strength in all our relationships—

personal and professional—the women's network will grow and prosper. And in the future there won't be any Queen Bees because there won't be any need for a woman to feel she has been engaged in a lonely, thankless battle, with countless enemies, real and imagined. In dealing from strength, we realize that asking for help is not admitting failure and offering help is not a power play.

Friends in Crisis

It's always good, life-enriching, and life-supporting to have friends. But in times of crisis you really need your friends to help you get through. They help you because they care. You let them help because in the end, you know that you will take responsibility, but you need to lean a little for a while. A crisis can be a tragedy or trauma, a time of great stress, great change, or major upheaval in your life.

All the women we spoke to had had some kind of stressful periods or periods of great change in their lives when friends were critical to their well-being—not their survival; these women would have survived somehow, but the quality of their getting through difficult times largely depended on the support and caring of their friends.

For Cathy, friends were supportive through the suicide of her first husband, leaving her with two small children to raise, the divorce of her second husband, and the emotional problems of her eldest son which led him into crime. Through it all, friends asked, "How can I help?"

For Rebecca, friends were there during her divorce and through her difficult period of reentry into the job market. Professionally they counseled her on possible jobs in her field of journalism. Personally they gave her support in the new life she was building for herself and her daughter. And she could also take encouragement from the examples of friends who had gone through before what she went through at the time. In that way friends can serve as role models for each other, as a reference point. A women may choose not to imitate the way a friend got through a difficult period, but she can use her example as a departure point: "This is how Ann handled it and survived. How do I want to deal with it?"

Helping friends through a crisis is a reciprocal thing. You help them; they help you. And we stress the word *help*. Real friends help each other in times of crisis, but they don't solve each other's problems. Even though all the women we spoke to relied on the support and help of their friends, they all agreed that they had to take control of their own lives and problems. Friends could help, but it was only beneficial when they themselves knew what to do in a given situation and wanted to be in control of whatever changes were taking place.

"No one can do it for you," says Karen. "The final decision—to cope or not to cope—is entirely up to you. It just won't work to try to place the full burden of your problems on one friend or several. It's unfair to them, and it's all wrong for you. You ultimately have to be in charge because your life is your responsibility."

Central to Karen's point is that friends will gladly give all the help they can to someone who is helping herself. But we've all had experiences with people who see themselves as perennial victims. They call to tell us their problems, but they haven't a clue to their solution. In fact, they never mention solutions. They are looking for sympathy, pure and simple, and actively avoid taking responsibility. These are the people who want to plug into your energy without putting any of their own energy into dealing with a crisis. You offer solutions; they give you ten reasons why none of the solutions will work, their situation is hopeless, ain't it awful?

Avoid energy-draining people. It's a particularly tricky trap for women who are in control of their lives because they are used to taking charge of a situation and sometimes miss the warning signals when an energy drainer is about to plug into them for life, if she's allowed to. As much as you may feel you should solve problems for another person, resist the temptation for two reasons. First, whether or not you realize it at the time, total responsibility for someone else's life is a drain on you. You're taking on a burden that doesn't belong to you, that will take your time and effort away from your own pursuits. You can't be a Mother Earth Problem Solver to the world. You can help, counsel, support, and advise, but you can't assume the burdens of other grown-ups.

Secondly, it's detrimental to the very person you're trying to help—the victim who refuses to accept responsibility. Key to her refusal to accept responsibility is the notion—conscious or unconscious—that someone else will provide, someone else will get her through. If you oblige, you confirm her view that she can be dependent on others for her survival. If she maintains that view and continues to act on it, she'll be an emotional cripple for her whole life. And as you will begin to resent her for draining your energy, she will begin to resent you for having all the answers. You have ceased to deal from strength with each other and taken on a sort of master/slave or mother/daughter relationship. The friendship is doomed.

And the consequences for both of you can be serious. If you make a practice of being Mother Earth Problem Solver for all takers, you will find yourself a counselor without portfolio (or pay) for the world at large. Your own goals will become secondary to "rescuing" victims who ought to be rescuing themselves. For the victim, the world becomes a scary place where only the intervention of some all-powerful, all-knowing other person can tell her what to do. Do yourself and a seeking victim a favor by refusing the role of Mother Earth Problem Solver.

The Perennial Victim

The perennial victim is the extreme case of someone unwilling to cope with her life. There are people who, from time to time, will dump a problem in your lap and ask you to solve it or play some major role in its solution. You have to judge each situation as it comes up, but our rule of thumb is reserve this kind of assistance for your very best friends or for family. As many daughters have found out as they get older, sometimes their mothers—and even their fathers—want a kind of role reversal in which the child becomes the parent. If you need to fulfill this role for one or both of your parents—in times of illness or family crisis—you may want to avoid other situations in which you will be called upon to solve problems. Remember that even a positive quality such as nurturing has its limits, and learn to say no without guilt when unfair demands are being made upon you.

Donna, a free-lance writer, wife, and mother to two growing sons, had a problem with energy drainers. She solved it by admitting that she was allowing people to drain her energy with their problems, and she took steps to correct her own actions so that they would be discouraged from calling her for help. She was receiving so many phone calls they were seriously interrupting her work. She went about breaking free in stages.

"First, I made excuses to people who were always calling for 'help.' I'd let the phone ring a couple of times while I decided whom I wanted to talk to," she said. "When I answered the phone, if the person on the other end was an energy drainer, I made some excuse, like 'I'm on my way out,' to cut the conversation short. Once I found I could do that, I escalated to 'I'm sorry I can't talk now. I've got work to finish' or 'I've got a deadline to meet.'

"Once I became comfortable with my new approach, I had this earthshaking revelation. The world would survive without me. All the people I thought were depending on me for their survival were able to cope on their own. It was a tremendous relief and freed a lot of the energy I wasn't even fully aware I was using to solve their problems."

If you can't say no to unnecessary phone interruptions, get an answering machine for your phone. The approaches can vary; the principle is the same: Conserve your energy for positive use on positive people.

Will Success Spoil the Career Woman?

If you're a smart career woman, you've already discovered the value of woman-to-woman friendships in the business world. You will have discovered it in spite of the fact that business does nothing to encourage women to become friends. If women do form friendships with one another in the same office, men tend to look at them as "the girls" and assume that they're gossiping, as women do, instead of networking and supporting, as women are learning to do. Still, if you've learned to enjoy the benefits of woman-to-woman friendships in your career, even when there are corporate obstacles, you know that the pluses far outweigh the minuses.

All that having been said, it would be naïve to assume that only sweetness and light will follow. Are there still women out there who resent the achievements of other women? You bet. And there will always be some people like that, men and women, but you don't have to choose them for friends. Envy is an ugly emotion, and it's a hurtful thing to be on the receiving end of another person's malice or ill will. But once you understand the motivation of envious people, you can discount their venom and feel sorry for them. Their thinking goes this way: "If she achieves X, somehow that diminishes me." That's nonsense on the face of it since we all have the opportunity to do what we want with our lives, so long as we are willing to put forth the time, effort, and talent necessary.

"Ever since I've become a manager, I've discovered that there are people out there—men and women—who resent me for having what they perceive is a powerful and glamorous job," Karen says. "They seem to forget that I put in twelve- to fourteen-hour days and that it's taken me more than twenty years to get where I am, that I've had to work my way up, and it hasn't been easy. My first reaction was shock, and I felt terribly hurt when a couple of people I thought were my friends were saying undercutting things behind my back. But after I got over the initial shock, I just learned to be wary, to look for people's ulterior motives. And I realize that the people who are envious of me would be envious of anyone in my position, so in that sense it's not personal. And it's really their problem because in the end, others know them for what they are."

If you are a woman on her way up, as you get promotions and raises and your career blossoms, some friendships may wither and die. Envy is one reason. Women who were helpful and supportive when you were young, inexperienced, and just starting out may feel threatened when you reach their level or move beyond them.

What can you do? You can either program yourself to fail to keep their friendship or realize that friends who don't wish you well in your success aren't worth having.

Some people play office politics, and women are not immune. You may find one or several women who like political games far more than they value friends. The trick is to discover these people early and avoid them. Above all, don't confide in them. Keep your networking and support for the women who will reciprocate in kind. Don't waste time with those who are out to score points with upper management—at your expense if you give them any ammunition. Eventually their scoring will get them nowhere, but in the short term they can be anything from a nuisance to a danger, so keep your relationship with them strictly business.

Aside from envy and politics, changing interests or responsibilities can cause office friends to drift. If you started out together as secretaries and you are now a supervisor or manager, your interests may be legitimately different. Your hours will very likely be different as well, since supervisors tend to work longer hours than secretaries. Take each friendship on an individual basis and see whether changing status—yours or your friend's—is affecting the friendship.

Would Your Mother Know You, If . . .

We *can* have some control over how our changing professional status may affect friendships. It can be pretty heady stuff to move up the corporate ladder and find yourself in a powerful and glamorous job. If you flaunt it, instead of just enjoying it, that can turn off the people who care about you. Keeping perspective on your professional success is your responsibility. It's good to remember that having a higher-level job doesn't necessarily make you a better person. You risk losing more than your friends if you lose who you are as a person in the process of becoming a business bigwig. You can easily lose yourself, and it's not easy to assemble the pieces again even if you later realize your mistake.

We asked all the women we interviewed whether their mothers would recognize them if they walked into their offices. The point is: Are they the same people at work as they are at home? Most answered yes, and we feel that's a significant point: that you are a person first and a career person second. If you are playing the role of a successful businesswoman, those who know you best and care about you most will see it. And they won't like it because it's not real; it's phony and contrived. You don't have to look and act like Joan Crawford just because you've entered the executive suite.

That having been said, it's true that as you work your way up, your job will become more high-powered, demanding fast, sometimes hard decisions. You'll have to pace yourself at work to deal with things in a crisply efficient way. There is often no time for small talk. If that's your situation, you may need to shift gears for friends even if they call you at the office. If you really don't have time to chat, say so nicely, and ask when it would be convenient for you to call them back. Or quickly set up a lunch or dinner date or make weekend plans with them and say, "I'd love to talk, but things are frenzied here, I've got to run." Friends will understand and will appreciate your good manners in letting them know. If you want people to understand your behavior, give them a frame of reference. We call this reading the situation. Let friends know your situation, and remember theirs. If you hear in their voices a call for help, take a minute and find out what's wrong; see if you can do anything right then to help. If they need to talk with you, arrange to meet them as quickly as possible even if it means rearranging your schedule. A good friend wouldn't call you with a problem if it weren't important. If your work situation isn't conducive to getting personal phone calls, let your friends know that, and tell them where and when they can reach you.

We have jobs in which our lunchtime is used mostly for business. Although we sometimes make lunch dates with friends, we let them know in advance that something may come up and we'll have to cancel for a business date. If you tell friends something like this in advance, they are much more likely to understand if and when the situation arises. Luckily we have friends who have the same kind of work schedule, so that the understanding that lunch plans can change at the last minute is mutual.

Sometimes the best way to get together if you and your friends are on tight schedules is to call each other on the spur of the moment to see whether lunch or dinner is free. Often same-day plans can work out where long-range ones can't. As with all aspects of having it all, you need to analyze your own work and personal situation and figure out the best method for coping.

One other possible pitfall to avoid: talking *ad nauseam* about your job with your friends. As fascinating as your work may be to you, as interesting as the cast of characters may be to you, the day-to-day details of other people's work are just not that interesting. Talking about high points—interesting or exciting things that have happened or about the fascinating people you've met—is fine, but regaling friends with the blow-by-blow account of your workday is bound to put them to sleep. And if you're in touch with yourself, it should put you to sleep as well. After all, friends are for sharing with, and you've got more to share than your work, haven't you?

If your friend happens to be a co-worker, more talk about the job is okay. For one thing, you have the same frame of reference. For another, you can give each other support and even guidance. But if you don't have that common ground, share work experiences selectively. Not only will your friends be happier with you, but you'll be happier with them since one of the things you look for in friendship is understanding. If you talk about work issues they can relate to, they can give you feedback and understanding and learn something themselves.

One of the most enjoyable evenings Joyce had was talking to a friend of a friend in Akron. The woman—we'll call her Ann—taught special education in Ohio and was discussing "her kids." She talked about their personalities, their problems, the parents who were helpful and those who didn't have the slightest understanding of the children's physical or mental limitations. As she spoke, her love for her students and her sense of commitment came through. At the end of the evening not only had Joyce learned a lot about an area that she hadn't had any contact with, but she came away with a tremendous sense of the kind of involvement Ann had in her work and how much love she brought to it.

How Success Can Poison a Friendship

If, at this point, you're wondering whether success has spoiled you or at least made life more difficult for you and your friends, perhaps it would be best to perform some mental exercises to see where you stand. What follow are some of the classic conflicts in career women friendships. You may see yourself or people close to you in these situations; if so, take the time to sort out your feelings about these conflicts, about the values of friendship you hold dear, and about your personal relationships in terms of your career.

1. You and your best office friend have worked side by side to make a project successful. It's paid off, the president of the company is ecstatic—and gives her the promotion and you a pat on the back. Of course, you're happy for your friend, but you're sad for yourself, and it's hard to keep on smiling when you've just been left in the dust.

2. You break your own rule and discuss your salary with a woman co-worker. What harm can it do? you think. You find out the next day when your mutual boss calls you in. He's livid because you've violated a confidence. She makes less than you do for the same job, she's just confronted him with your salary, and now he's in a bind.

3. You've been friends ever since you went to college. You've compared career notes for the last eight years as you've moved up the corporate ladder in your respective fields. Suddenly you're both making good salaries. And suddenly your lunches become exercises in one-upmanship as you discuss your new mink and she

shows you pictures of her eight-room co-op, you discuss your trip to the South of France and she shows you the diamond ring she just bought herself. You used to be comrades, but now you're competitors.

4. You and Sally have been friends since you climbed the apple tree together when you were eight. You both wanted careers, but she got married right out of high school and, three kids later, feels trapped. You, on the other hand, have a successful career, and it seems that no problem is too big for you to solve. So Sally tells you all her problems, waiting trustingly for you to solve them. You begin to feel like Atlas holding up the world and want to shrug her problems off your shoulders and back onto hers, but you know if you do, she'll look at you accusingly.

5. You and Jane have worked so well together at ABC Corporation you decide to go into partnership and make money for yourselves. The only problem is you're two chiefs with no Indians. Each of you wants to be boss. In ABC Corporation each of you had her own domain. Now you're sharing one, and you can't seem to decide who makes the final decisions—nor can you agree on final decisions when you try to make them jointly.

6. You've known Cathy since you started with the company five years ago. In fact, you began together as secretaries. Cathy's still a secretary, but you're now a supervisor. And your first job, according to your boss, is to fire Cathy. You know he's right, she just hasn't been doing the job, but still, she's your friend, your oldest friend in the company, and you know your friendship won't survive your firing her. Watching an old Joan Crawford movie the night before may help, but we doubt it.

Having Friends of the Opposite Sex

Now that we've talked about women's relationships with women, there's another positive area open to career women today: the ability to form friendships with men in the business world— not dating relationships or sexual relationships, but friendships. What are the benefits of friendships with people of the same sex?

What are the benefits of friendships with people of the opposite sex?

When your friends are of the same sex, you start out with one basic thing in common: your sexual identity. You are women together, sharing the same physiology and some of the same experiences and perspectives as women. Having the same sex in common isn't a sufficient basis for friendship, but it's a common starting ground. As career women you can share work experiences and what led you to a career; you can discuss problems for women in a field or progress that's been made. Most women feel freer to talk to another woman about deep feelings or sexual feelings, fantasies, or problems than they do to men.

There's something unique about friendship with someone of your own sex—a connection that's more than biology. It is perhaps that common perspective, even if each woman's approach to life may be very different.

But if relationships with members of your own sex offer a special, unique feeling, so do relationships between women and men. Women getting out into the work force have made it easier for men and women to be friends—just friends, with no innuendos or gossip from their peers. Because they meet and work together naturally, they get to know each other in a nonthreatening situation. If they are co-workers, the man doesn't feel compelled to make a pass, as he might if he were meeting her in a singles bar or at a party, and the woman doesn't feel wary that she will have to fend off a pass at any moment.

Yes, people who meet in the office have affairs. Some even fall in love and get married. But there are others who make friends. And men and women have learned the joys of friendship with the opposite sex.

For women, it's a chance to share the world from a male perspective, to see his viewpoints. Professionally it might open up to her areas she's not familiar with in his business because his experiences have been different. For men, having a friendship with a woman may allow them to be more open about their feelings than their friendships with men allow. They may be able to talk about their fears, their vulnerability, and their gentleness, receiving supportive feedback and admiration that assure them it's all right for men to have these feelings.

If neither one is involved in a special relationship, they can "date" each other in a friendly way, providing companionship and shared fun and new experiences. They can trade on each other's strengths and help shore up each other's weaknesses.

Friends and the Man in Your Life

Although the man in your life may be the closest, most important person to you, friends are still important for sharing. No two people can share everything, all the time, to the same degree. Friends are the support system with which you share those issues, feelings, and experiences that your mate may not be interested in or may not be interested in to the same degree that you are. You may even discuss some of the same issues and feelings with friends that you discuss with your mate, for a different perspective or emphasis.

If you have chosen a mate for life, in some ways you are a unit: You live together, make joint plans for the future, have a day-to-day intimate context that friends don't share. On the other hand, although you may function in many ways as a unit, you are two individuals whose needs are not always the same, and that's where friends as support systems enrich your life. You may have some friends who are separate, some friends who are mutual. They add to your primary relationship; they don't detract.

You need to be sensitive to each other's needs and expectations where friends are concerned.

For example, when Joyce sees her childhood friend Susan, they like to spend a couple of hours alone together getting caught up on what's happening to the friends they grew up with. Peter might join them for dinner but would rather leave the two of them alone to reminisce about people he doesn't know. On the other hand, Peter loves to golf and fish and has a group of friends with whom he pursues these activities. Joyce sees this as a plus. He gets to pursue his hobbies, and she gets to pursue hers, which don't include fishing and golfing.

One of the keys to having it all is to spread out your expectations, your needs, and your interests to the community of loving, caring people you have in your life—mate, friends, and family.

You can see the successful life as a progression of building blocks. First, you get to know, understand, and accept yourself. Next, you branch out to find and nurture friends who will be supportive and caring. Next, you look for a romantic relationship that will be lasting and loving, the beginning of your own family unit, whether it's a unit of two, three, four, five, whatever, should you choose to have children or not.

In this chapter, we've discussed friendships because after the knowing of yourself, the ability to choose and nurture friends who will have a positive effect on your life is the most important next step to having it all. If you can successfully branch out to share your goals and values with people who are like you, who understand you, you're well on your way to being a fulfilled person. And you're ready for the next step—the man in your life.

FOUR

WHEN YOU
HAVE A MAN
IN YOUR LIFE

There's no one man in my life right now, but there are a couple of men that I see who are really friends, who know me very well, who are great to be with until the one, right person comes along. I know I haven't met that person yet, and I know if I had to, I could survive very well alone, but I'd like for the future to have one man to share my life with.

We knew each other almost six years before we got married. It took that long for both of us to settle into our careers, settle into our lives, and know we were right for each other. We met in our twenties, and in that sense, we almost grew up together.

Luckily we grew together and not apart. Now that we're married, we both feel really happy and comfortable. The day-to-day mechanics of the relationship haven't really changed, but the sense of long-term commitment is there now, and it adds a lot to the way we both feel.

Sam is not only my husband but my best friend. I can talk to him about everything. We love to share things. We never seem to have enough time alone, just to enjoy each other, what with his work and mine. But we manage to find time. We jog together, play music together. He loves to read articles I've written, and I love to hear his comments. We're both very oral: We love to talk; we love to kiss; we love to eat. We always talk everything out, even when we have a problem. My first marriage was a disaster, but my second marriage has really brought more pleasure into my life. I think it's because I'm a happier person now than when I married the first time.

I really love Jack, but I don't know that I'll ever marry him. He's been married before and doesn't seem ready for commitment. I don't trust him. He's not consistent. I never know when he's going to turn up on my doorstep. Days or even weeks can go by without my hearing from him. Although he says he loves me, he sees other women, and he keeps talking about needing his freedom. I've been through one marriage and the death of my husband. I know what it's like to be alone, and I know I can handle it. And I'd rather be alone than married to someone like Jack, who can't really give of himself. Probably the answer is to look for someone new, someone who can be as committed as I can be.

CAREER WOMEN KNOW the value of dealing through strength in their lives. In business they must deal through strength to succeed. In Chapter Three we talked about dealing through strength in friendships, how important it is to choose and maintain friends who are independent, givers as well as takers, who exchange values with you instead of feeding off you. As important as dealing through strength is in all other areas of the career woman's life, it is even more critical in a relationship with a man, whether she is just seeing him all the time, is living with him, or is married to him.

Many of the women we interviewed were in their second marriages, and most cited not dealing through strength as the issue that had made their marriages come unglued. Either they weren't independent enough to know what they wanted and ask for it, or the man they had chosen couldn't deal with an equal partner. Those who had married for a second time had consciously chosen an equal, someone whose strength matched theirs.

If you're ambitious, serious about your work, strong in your values and what you want out of life, you need a partner who reflects these traits—or your personalities will grate against each other, and the fabric of the relationship will shred. We're not talking here about temperamental differences—one mate can be outgoing and talkative, and the other shy and introverted—but the inner strength should be equal. We're not even talking about who makes more money—some professions pay more than others, and there are other motivations for working in life than just a paycheck. What we are talking about is the desire to be good, to succeed, to be in control of your life, to be independent. Unless couples are evenly matched in this area, a career woman's relationship with a man can be fraught with difficulties.

Once you have a real relationship between two equals, everything else can work, even when compromise is necessary, or there are disagreements—so long as you know that the other person can stand on his own two feet, that you can independently pursue your goals, and that you will choose joint goals together.

One woman commented wryly to us, "I'll get married on the day that one of those countless men who've told me, 'Lean on me, lean on me,' doesn't fall over when I just rest my head on his shoulder. I still haven't met a man who can cope as well as I can, and I won't get married until I do."

When you deal through strength with your man, the positive emotions flow. You are proud of each other, admire each other, have mutual trust and respect, affection, and companionship as well as love. Those positive feelings are reinforced as you see each other living your lives as independent, productive people. The foundation you build with these positive emotions is strong enough to sustain not only the minor upheavals of life but the major ones as well.

Many of us have not always dealt through strength in our relationships with men. For one thing, mother taught us to pretend to admire a man even when we didn't. As we've learned to be honest about ourselves, we've learned to look honestly at the men we love. If we have to pretend any positive emotions, we end up denying ourselves and our own values. And that's hardly a climate in which love can thrive.

When you deal through strength, you can defer to each other, leave decisions in each other's hands, because you know whichever of you makes a specific decision, he or you will be in control of the situation. If only one of you is in control, there can be no sharing of responsibilities. That's a one-way exchange, with one partner becoming the energy source and the other becoming the energy drainer. The career women we talked to who felt their marriages worked talked about a flow of positive energy between them and their husbands. That's the key.

Wonder Woman at the Office, Silly Putty at Home

From nine to five, or six, or seven, you delegate tasks, meet deadlines, solve problems—in short, you are in charge; you are in control. After that, you shift gears to become—whom?

When Joyce was working for the Gannett Newspapers in Westchester, New York, a very successful woman editor came to her one day and said, "My husband's just summed up my mind set.

He asked me last night, 'How can you be Wonder Woman at the office and Silly Putty at home?' "

It struck Joyce as a particularly perceptive comment. Having control, power—whatever term you want to use—all day long can work two ways on a woman. She can go home wanting to maintain that control, or she can "cave in," becoming Silly Putty because her husband is there to take care of things.

Wanting to maintain unilateral control can be disastrous. After all, being part of a couple is a joint venture, so the Wonder Woman approach doesn't work. But becoming Silly Putty is confusing—not only to your mate but to you.

All of this brings us to the principle of Shifting Gears. At work, you assume one role; at home, you assume another. However, you are still the same person. So how do you adapt your behavior from one situation to another?

Bettye and Charlie drive home from the office together every night. She uses that time to shift gears, to go from corporate recruiter to wife and mother. She slows down the pace, talking with Charlie about his day and hers. By the time they reach home they've shifted their focus to their family life. The ride takes only fifteen minutes, but Bettye has learned to shift her gears in that amount of time.

Susan, who is single, says she finds it difficult to make this transition. Outwardly she's on a date. Inside, she's still go, go, go. "What do you do when you want to shift gears but you find your clutch isn't working?" she asked.

We told her to get a new clutch—or at least a new approach to winding down at the end of the day. Things like yoga, meditation, and jogging help some people to relax. If you find yourself too wound up at the end of the day to shift gears into the private you, examine your job and your inner attitudes toward it. If it's making you into a nervous wreck, change jobs. If your attitude is just too hyper, try to slow it down and calm down. You need to relax, regroup, see that other side of your life. If your husband wants to take care of you a little, relax and enjoy it. If he wants to be taken care of a little, indulge him. We all need to be nurtured and taken care of from time to time even when we know we can do the specific thing ourselves. Part of being liberated is having the inner confidence to know you can do something, so you don't have to prove it by doing it yourself every time.

The Bottom Line in Relationships

How do you know when a romantic relationship is right for you? In one sense, there are as many answers to that question as there are people. But in the context of career women, there are certain necessary conditions or factors for a romantic relationship to be the positive, nurturing part of your life you want it to be.

Mutual understanding is a must. It used to be traditional that it was a wife's job to understand her husband. No one ever spoke about the husband's understanding the wife. After all, he was out earning the living. She was supposed to make a home for him and give him all the emotional fuel and strength he needed to go out there and tackle the world day after day. Now both of you are out there tackling the world, and the understanding needs to be mutual. By understanding, we mean knowing what makes a person tick, what motivates him or her at the base of it all. As a career woman you have a life independent of the man in your life, but you also have a life with him. Does he understand the total you? Does he understand your goals and aspirations, your needs, your plans for the future? Do you understand his? Understanding leads to tolerance and acceptance of each other's actions and priorities. Without understanding, you'll both be confused, hurt, frustrated, angry, or bewildered most of the time.

Once you know that you have mutual understanding, does mutual support follow? It's one thing to understand why your mate does what he does, but do you approve and agree? Do you feel good about cheering him on? And does he feel supportive of you?

Donna told us that if her husband, Louis, hadn't understood how important it was for her to write, she doesn't know what would have happened to her marriage or her writing. With two small children to care for, Donna could easily have got caught up in her day-to-day existence and lost sight—at least in the short term —of her writing goal. But Louis knew that writing was part of Donna, and he wanted her to have work of her own that gave her a sense of fulfillment. He encouraged her in every way possible, from helping with household and baby-sitting chores to financing trips for free-lance articles she would do on speculation. Now that the children are older, Donna has a staff job writing full time, but it couldn't have happened without Louis's support.

Another friend—we'll call her Molly—told us that when she lost her job, her husband, Fred, really helped her get through the first twenty-four hours. "It was silly in a way that I got so upset when I was fired," Molly says two years later. "Half my department was let go on the same day, the result of a corporate power struggle. I hadn't even been enjoying the job for the last year or so because of the politics. But I had never been fired before, and I really took it to heart. Fred said to me, 'Tomorrow you'll realize this is the best thing that's ever happened to you. You'll find something more rewarding that you really enjoy. If you don't find something rght away, you can stay home for a while. I can support you. Just know that you're free to choose what you want to do next.' That meant so much to me, knowing that I had his support. And of course, he was right. Twenty-four hours later I did realize it was the best thing to have happened."

Just as you need support from your friends, you need support from the man in your life—even more so, since he is a primary value, whereas some friends may be of secondary value to you.

A third element you need to look for in a romantic relationship is friendship. Forget those old love songs that wail, "I love her, but I don't like her." Long-term relationships begin with a man and a woman liking each other, being friends with each other. Of course, understanding and support are part of friendship. So is sharing—of time, money, effort, plans, values, friends, interests. The women we interviewed who are happily married said they had lots in common with their husbands. When we asked them what they talked about together, most of them said, "Everything." When we asked them if they had best friends, frequently they said their husbands were.

A solid romantic relationship needs consistency. Just as you've worked to know yourself and to be yourself in all situations, you want a mate who can do the same. People who are warm one day, cold the next, supportive one minute and indifferent the next do nothing to nurture you. Mostly they confuse and hurt you. Grown-ups are consistent. They don't find anything interesting or mysterious in being "strange" or unpredictable. At the beginning of a romance it may be fun to wait for a man to call, never knowing when—or if—he will. But if you're married and you still don't know when he'll call, mystery turns into uncertainty and inconsistency. You've worked hard to be in control of your life. Try being in control with an inconsistent mate. You can't make plans; you can't count on anything but his inconsistency. Save the allure of the mystery man for your fantasies.

Another combination of qualities you need for a successful relationship is chemistry and trust. You need chemistry—or excitement, passion, a feeling of coming home when you're with another person because otherwise, you'll get bored. And with the options open to career women, there'll be other men out there to relieve your boredom if you don't have excitement at home. If there's no chemistry, the relationship won't last—or at least it won't last as an open, honest, one-on-one relationship. Once you know you've got chemistry flowing between you, you need to trust each other. For starters, you trust each other not to cheat. In the 1960s, as part of the sexual revolution, it became fashionable to cheat. Or so people thought at the time. Husband-and-wife authors George and Nena O'Neill advocated "outside relationships" in their best-seller *Open Marriage*. Interestingly enough, their next book on marriage, *The Marriage Premise*, written a decade later, recanted that advice. Trust and one-to-one relationships were still valid and important, they'd discovered. Most people who have good, happy marriages will tell you the same thing. You don't cheat, and you trust that your partner won't either.

Of course, trust goes beyond cheating. Really, you trust someone to be true and loyal to you in all areas, not just sexually. You trust your mate's judgment, his goodwill, his interest in what's best for you, his honesty and integrity, his fiscal responsibility.

Other elements to look for in a romantic relationship are, of course, love, a sense of companionship, a sense of humor, and perspective to get you through difficult times with a laugh and to heighten your enjoyment of the good times. Thoughtfulness and caring are important. The bottom line: Does the relationship add to your life or take away from it? Are you heightened or diminished as a person by the relationship? Are you proud of the man you've chosen, and does he reflect your values?

Choosing the right man with whom to share your life is never easy. Even the man who sweeps you off your feet initially may not wear well over the long term. For a career woman, it can be an even more difficult choice to make because she needs to find a man who is as secure, flexible, and understanding as she is. We've prepared a quiz that offers some guidelines on what to look for. The questions are divided into three categories: security, flexibility, and interest. If you can answer yes to most of the questions, you've probably found Mr. Right. If you have more no than yes answers, you may want to take a second look at the man in your life or at least renegotiate the ground rules.

I. SECURITY: *How secure is he in his role?*

	Yes	No
1. There would be a celebration if I got a $10,000 raise.		
2. He speaks well of the professional women in his own office and works well with them.		
3. When he is with his male friends, he never makes apologies for the fact that I am very involved in my career.		
4. He gives me emotional support when I experience a setback in my career. He never uses my vulnerable moments to show off as a macho man.		

	Yes	No

5. He willingly escorts me to the business functions I have to attend.

6. When it looks as if I am moving faster toward my career goals than he is, he is not threatened or envious; he's proud of me and confident that his turn will come.

7. He likes to tell his family about my career and my accomplishments.

8. I never feel I have to play down an achievement because he will feel hurt or jealous.

9. When I ask him if he could ever work for a woman boss, he answers, "Of course."

10. He could (or does) accept the fact that I earn more than he does.

II. FLEXIBILITY: *How much is he willing to give?*

	Yes	No

1. My job requires some travel. He understands and accepts it and never makes me feel guilty for leaving him alone.

2. He accepts the running of the household as a shared chore, not as a source of resentment because if I weren't working, I could handle all the chores and he wouldn't have to bother.

3. We trade off tasks with ease when my hours or his go through peak periods.

4. There have been times when I have had business meetings that run into the evening, and a male colleague will say, "Let's finish this over a drink." He trusts me to handle myself as a professional, and there are no undercurrents of jealousy.

5. When he has a problem with something I'm doing, he knows when and how to approach me

	Yes	No

about it, and we can discuss it calmly, without having a fight.

6. He understands clearly the difference between professional friendships and social friendships and respects how I handle the two.

7. If we both have had bad days, he doesn't always have to talk about his first but realizes that there needs to be an equal give-and-take.

8. He doesn't expect me always to be the one to make the traditionally female decisions, such as social plans, assigning the housework, handling household help, choosing schools for the children, etc. He likes to participate.

III. INTEREST: *How much does he care about whether you succeed?*

	Yes	No

1. He doesn't fake interest in my career just to appease me. I know he really cares.

2. At the end of the day, he knows what questions to ask to draw me out and knows when I need to talk and when I don't.

3. We talk often about job stress, and he understands that I go through the same things he does.

4. At a party he genuinely likes to talk about my career interests as well as his own. He doesn't feel threatened if my situation is more interesting than his to the outside world.

5. When he sees an article in a professional journal or newspaper that he feels I should read, he points it out, and we discuss it. And vice versa.

6. My business trips interest him, and we often talk about them in some detail when I get home.

	Yes	No
7. He has no problem either giving advice or listening to constructive criticism regarding either of our career situations.	___	___
8. If he should have the opportunity to introduce me to an influential person in my field, he would recognize the opportunity and take advantage of it.	___	___

Among the three categories there are a total of twenty-six questions. Count your yes answers, and put the total here: _____.

If your total is above fourteen, it sounds as if you've found a man who can deal with a career woman. We suggest you keep him.

If your total is less than fourteen, take a closer look at the man in your life. You may have a potential problem on your hands.

Marriage, Career, and Divorce

Not every relationship lives happily ever after. The divorce rate can discourage even the most hopeful person; nearly one in every two marriages ends in divorce in the United States. On the other hand, more and more people are getting married, and second marriages have become common.

Many of the women we interviewed have been divorced. We have been through marriages that didn't work. In the debate that still goes on in society, many people have questioned whether women's having careers—being "liberated"—will destroy the fabric of marriage and the family. Of course, it's very convenient for those who oppose careers for women to see them as interfering with being married or being a mother.

In our cases, our marriages did not end because we had careers. Joyce was married at twenty to a very good man who was simply not right for her. The major factor in the breakup of the marriage was her age: She had not been mature enough to choose a mate for a lifetime. When she realized that, the best solution was to end it. It was an amicable divorce, and her husband had been extremely supportive and proud of her career. They are friends to this day.

In Bettye's case, she and her husband simply grew apart, and they discovered when Bettye became pregnant that even on this issue they couldn't agree. He didn't want children, so in Bettye's case she chose motherhood instead of a marriage that was already troubled.

With the women we interviewed who were divorced, a couple of them did feel that their careers were major factors in the breakup of their marriages. For Sherry, her husband's traditional view that the man should be the breadwinner was a tremendous source of friction in her marriage. He wanted her to be Mrs. Sidney Greene. She wanted to be Ms. Sherry Greene, with a career of her own. He felt that her working made it look as if he couldn't afford to support her. After all, his friends' wives spent their days at the country club while Sherry was out working.

When we talked about dealing through strength in a relationship, we mentioned mutual understanding as being crucial. Obviously Sidney didn't understand Sherry's desire to have a career, and she didn't want a life as just Sidney's wife, so the marriage ended.

Judy's marriage ended because her husband felt he couldn't compete with her success. She had a better position than he, made more money, seemed more in control of her life. He sought refuge in an affair with another woman, and when Judy found out and confronted him, he blamed her independence for making him feel inadequate. Again, the issue of dealing through strength comes up— it was not a marriage of equals, as Judy says now, and she chose for a second husband a man who is every bit as successful as she is.

Having a career makes any person more independent, more complex, with more varied interests. Because of those things, a person begins to define more clearly what he or she wants in all areas of life. For a woman today, marriage is not the ticket to security that it may have been for her mother's generation. It's a sharing of a life, including the incomes both make, and for the career woman, it's a sharing of the lives of two people with un-limited options. Therefore, a marrage may come under closer scrutiny because the woman's values are more clearly defined.

When two people in a marriage or relationship have careers, it adds an extra dimension. Scheduling and the division of day-to-day household chores become more complex; roles become blurred from the traditional standards. Flexibility is needed by both partners to make their lives work.

Discussing together potential areas of conflict and deciding how you want to handle them can defuse a lot of these issues. And feelings should be talked about as well. Hiding behind that career woman image may be the childhood feelings of a housewife and homemaker. You may have your own ambivalences about being a working wife. Hiding behind that façade of liberated manhood may be childhood feelings of wanting to be the macho breadwin-ner, and your husband may have ambivalent feelings about your having a career. Only by airing your true feelings can real under-standing take place.

Above and beyond any sensitive areas that may arise because it is a two-career marriage or relationship, any marriage takes work to run smoothly. Think of any of the people you know who have been happily married for a long time. We're sure they've mentioned that they work at their marriages, that they try to stay flexible, to understand each other's needs and feelings, to be there for each other in times of crisis, to tolerate quirks in a loved one that they'd never tolerate in someone else. And they know the value of com-promise in a relationship in which both partners have needs and each has to give a little to satisfy the other. They've probably also mentioned a sense of humor—being able to laugh at some of the problems that seemed so big at the time but were so easily resolved.

If a marriage or relationship is really important to you—if it's one of your top priorities—then the compromises you may have to make over the years to make it work will be worth it, and you'll make them willingly because you know it's important.

Probably the key to a successful marriage is knowing yourself and your needs and choosing a partner who reflects them. We call this the Mirror Principle. If you're comfortable and happy with who you are, if you like and accept yourself, then the man you choose will be a reflection of your attitudes and views. Of course, this cuts two ways. If you're unsure of yourself, are ambivalent about your role—traditional woman versus career woman—then the man you choose will be likely to reflect those ambivalences as well. Or worse, you may play one role to get him—that of the traditional woman—and be trapped inside it for the duration of your marriage because that's what he wanted in the first place and that's what you offered him.

In Chapter Two we talked about the importance of self-knowledge before branching out into other relationships. In friendships, but especially in romantic relationships, self-knowledge determines whether your relationships with others will be successful. You need to know who you are before you're fully able to know and understand someone else. If you're not sure of who you are, don't depend on a relationship to give you the answers. When women had no sense of an independent identity, they would often look to men to define them, to "make them happy." It didn't work then, and it won't work now. You can't depend on someone else to "make you happy" if you don't define for yourself what gives you happiness. A relationship isn't a separate entity; it's the coming together of two independent people. As such, it will be only as good as the sum of its two parts. If you wait for a relationship to transform you, you'll wait your whole life away, and it will never happen. Realistic expectations going in are critical to achieving any goal in life, and a successful, rewarding romantic relationship is no exception.

The Fine Art of Sharing

Marabel Morgan notwithstanding, marriage and career are totally compatible for women. First of all, they've been totally compatible for men for centuries—surely the sexes aren't that different! Even Mrs. Morgan has a career—she gives lectures and sponsors seminars around the country, counseling women on how to be fulfilled by staying at home and caring for their husbands. By her own admission, her marriage is thriving.

The majority of career women we interviewed for this book are married. We are married. Having said it can work, we also admit that dual-career marriages need the same elements as the rest of your life to be successful: planning, organization, clear setting of goals, follow-through, understanding, and flexibility. Of course, the same principles apply to dual-career couples who live together without being married. What we're really talking about is two people who are committed to each other. A good relationship is really the application of the Fine Art of Sharing.

Being committed is no small thing. It means sticking together in good times and bad, figuring out the problems as they occur, and solving them. But being committed isn't just a series of problems to solve. Ideally it's a tremendous opportunity for two people to grow together, to set independent and joint goals, to plan long range and see the plans through.

Most of the women we interviewed who have men in their lives said over and over again that the men were understanding of their jobs and the demands made on their time and energy. They were willing to help, from splitting mundane chores to being supportive. Unless you're one of those rare career women with a nine-to-five schedule, you're going to have to find a man who understands when occasionally—or perhaps, for a period of time, regularly—you're not home for dinner. And of course, that understanding needs to be reciprocated. You have to give to get.

You need to have life values and long-term goals in common. Yes, these can change or be modified, but at the root of things, you need to be going in the same direction. For example, if you want nothing more than to write romantic novels in a charming house in the woods and he wants to be president of a company located in a major city, with all the social events and entertaining that will entail, at some point you're going to have major conflict. A large part of having it all is knowing who you are and what your needs are, then finding the man who reflects those needs.

Finding Time to Be Alone Together

All the women we interviewed with men in their lives said they consciously plan time to be alone together. Just as each person needs time to be alone, a couple needs time to be alone together to recharge the batteries of their relationship, to share things privately, without outside, day-to-day hassles intruding.

People find time to be alone together in a number of ways. Some couples plan to go out to dinner alone one or two nights a week, or they have a romantic dinner at home. That's a little trickier because you have either to take the phone off the hook or to be pleasant but firm with any callers, saying that you're busy and can't talk. If you have an intrusive boss who regularly calls you at home or a mother who calls daily "just to see how you are," take the phone off the hook or go out.

Other couples plan regular getaway weekends. Some buy or rent country homes; others just choose spots that appeal to them. How often you do it is really a personal and practical choice. How often can you afford it? How regularly can you schedule it? There are certain guidelines. Once a year is not enough. Neither is twice a year. Three times a year is a bare minimum. Monthly is heaven.

Vacations are a must. They need to be taken at least once a year and preferably for at least two weeks at a time—one week barely gives you time to know you're on vacation before it's time to return. Vacations give couples the opportunity to see and experience new things together, to communicate in a relaxed atmosphere, to see each other in new ways in new situations.

Other couples keep one day of every weekend as a day to spend together. They may do nothing more exciting than read the Sunday papers. Judy and George love to do the Sunday *Times*'s crossword puzzle together. In the summer they play softball at their summer house.

Bettye and Charlie use their country house as a retreat from their busy lives. They pack up the children, the maid, and the dog and leave the city far behind.

The secret to making sure you get time alone together is to

put it at the top of the list of your personal priorities. We both are list makers and have found it really helps to put down on paper what's important to you, then to act accordingly. If you don't schedule alone time, you'll find you won't have it. Something else will come up.

One thing that can happen to two career people in a relationship is that they sometimes forget to listen to each other. Here's the scenario: Each of you comes home at the end of the day, full of your experiences—good or bad, they just happened, and probably you want to share some of them or all of them. You come home to a person who's had the same kind of experiences and may want to talk about them, too. Result: You talk at each other, and no real exchange takes place.

There are almost as many ways to get around this problem as there are people.

Bettye and Charlie almost never discuss work at home. Joyce and Peter discuss it, with the understanding that if either one of them gets too boring or long-winded, the topic is switched. Judy likes to have at least an hour alone when she gets home at night so that she can put the day behind her, unwind, and be ready to talk to George about nonwork topics. Rebecca and Sam share their work. She will read him a piece she's written, he will show her photographs he's taken, but they don't rehash their day.

If the problem of talking at each other gets out of hand, it can become a contest of either "who's experienced more stress" or "who's had the greatest triumph." Like siblings vying for mama's attention, the couple can play "Can You Top This?" until one gives in and listens to the other—neither productive nor enjoyable.

Learning to Make Trade-offs

Even in marriages made in heaven, partners will disagree with one another. That's where learning to make trade-offs pays. You already know how to make trade-offs in other areas of your life. For example, you rent an apartment with a great view, even though it has a small kitchen, since the view is more important to you and you couldn't find an apartment that has both. Or you accept a job that may pay less but gets you in position for your next two career moves; the long-term goal outweighs the short-term disadvantage. In a marriage, trade-offs allow each partner independent joys and allow them to share interests. For example, he loves hockey, and you hate it. You love ballet, and he can't stand it. Most times you go to the ballet on the evenings he goes to the hockey game, but occasionally, for some special events, like the Stanley Cup Playoffs, you'll go with him, and he'll reciprocate when you want to see that performance of *Giselle*. You accompany each other to share a special interest. Your going to the hockey game makes your husband happy. And you're happy when he goes to the ballet. An unexpected fringe benefit may be that you find that hockey has its moments and he finds ballet isn't as boring as he thought.

The trick to making trade-offs is to be gracious about them. You compromise with a smile. Remember, part of loving another person is understanding his needs. If your doing something for him would make him very happy and you view it as a minor inconvenience to you, do it. Of course, he'll reciprocate. And you both get to appreciate each other's understanding and generosity. Another term for trade-offs in marriage is giving and getting love.

Even with friends, you may have to make compromises. Although most couples have some mutual friends, they also have friends that they see independently. You need to give each other time to pursue these independent friendships. You also need to be willing from time to time to see friends of his whom you wouldn't particularly pick out. And he should do the same for you.

Family can pose the same problems. You may really love to see your family a lot, and he may be interested in seeing them only occasionally, but he may go more often than he'd choose to because it gives you pleasure. And you would reciprocate. You would also do things for his family and yours that you wouldn't do for other people—like drive 500 miles to the family reunion or attend a niece or nephew's graduation, where you may have to stand in the heat and listen to five speeches, all of which say nothing. You do it because it's his family or yours. You may also have to put into perspective any prejudices or viewpoints that his family may have that you don't share. Sometimes it's hard for your husband's mother to understand why his wife would want to work instead of staying home to take care of him. Your understanding of her viewpoint will mean a lot to your husband. After all, she's his mother, and out of your love for him, you extend goodwill to her. He may reciprocate by allowing your father to tease him because he does the laundry.

Some couples are contending with this kind of family compromise on an ongoing basis in second marriages in which there are children from previous marriages. There will be more about how to solve these conflicts in Chapter Five, which is all about children and how they fit into having it all.

Whose Friends Are They Anyway?

As a couple, whose friends do you see? His friends? Your friends? Mutual friends?

Most of the women we talked to had strong connections with other women friends. They saw them regularly and shared many of the intimate details of their lives as well as feelings and attitudes. Most said their husbands did not have friends who were this close to them.

It's hardly surprising. If women have had to develop business skills, men are just at the beginning of learning how to form intimate, sharing relationships with one another. Culturally they have been taught to have "pals," to see the "boys." They talk or play sports. They discuss business or the state of the world. Or sex. They talk about everything but themselves, who they are and what they feel. As a consequence, most men don't form the open, caring kind of friendships that most women do.

So where does that leave you for socializing? For us and for most of the women we interviewed, socializing was done with their friends and their spouses. Their husbands didn't mind it. Most of the women make all the social arrangements, although they usually check them with their husbands, and the men seem to like having activities planned for them. Sometimes it has led to friendships among the men who have been brought together by their wives.

Even though all this sounds simple, it isn't. If you make friends at work, you may tend to discuss business even when you're with your spouses—a bore for them because they don't know the people or situations you're talking about. Bad for you because here you are in your leisure time discussing the Office. It looms large enough all day, five days a week. Why bring it home or take it out on a Saturday night with friends?

On the other hand, some friends you meet at work may share lots of your interests and those of your mate, and the chances are better for successful group socializing.

Sometimes a person you find fascinating is boring or, worse, irritating for your spouse to be around. Maintain that friendship on your own. There are enough people you can mutually enjoy.

With one exception: the business "friend" who is really a business "contact" or the boss, whose invitation is a command performance or at least obligatory. This is where a combination of firmness and flexibility can help.

Face it. You're going to have to accept a certain percentage of these invitations. You will probably even have to reciprocate them. If you like the people, it's painless, even enjoyable. If you'd prefer to keep business business, but they insist, explain the situation to your mate, ask him to do it for you, and tell him you owe him one.

At the same time you can limit the contact by making certain times off limits. For example, if your general policy is to stay home on weeknights, you can make one or two exceptions for the boss or contact, but let the person know, graciously, that you're making an exception and weeknights don't really work for you on a regular basis. Make sure that's the truth because people have a way of finding out whether or not it is. Or you might want to use the same strategy for weekends or for a certain day of the weekend.

There are some excuses that are acceptable. Illness, for example. But use it sparingly. A conflicting engagement or a personal project or activity can get you off the hook: "I'd love to come for the weekend. Nancy, but I play golf every Saturday, and it's really important to me to play with my foursome, so we just don't accept weekend invitations."

Since some people just don't distinguish between business and personal relationships, at some point, in some job, you'll be placed in the position of having to spend a certain number of hours with people you wouldn't pick out if the choice were up to you. You can control it by limiting it.

Will Marriage Change the Career Woman?

Marriage affects the career woman's business life in a couple of ways. If she has been living with a man without being married, in some fields—especially conservative ones like banking and insurance—her marriage will legitimize her, make her a traditional person in the eyes of her employer. On the other hand, marriage can be seen to reduce a woman's flexibility. The same employer who may find it more "respectable" for a woman to be married than living with someone might be even happier if she were just plain single.

For one thing, employers still think about women's getting pregnant. When a female employee gets married, the pregnancy issue can loom large even though the law prohibits employers from discussing it as an issue of employment and prohibits them from using it as grounds for firing or job discrimination. In their minds, a newly married woman today can be a pregnant woman a month from now. In Chapter Five we'll talk more about dealing with pregnancy when you have a career, including how to break the news to your boss.

Aside from the pregnancy issue, there are a couple of other issues that may make you seem less flexible to your employer. For one, if your company relocates people on a regular basis, your being married could be viewed as making relocation at least more difficult, if not impossible, since your husband's career has to be considered. Joyce worked for one woman boss (herself married) who viewed the marriage of any female on her staff as a catastrophe because she felt that a married woman would not want to work late into the evening and on weekends. Of course, the trick here is never to work for a workaholic or, married or single, your life wouldn't be your own. But if you know your boss has any kind of prejudice against married female employees, at least plan your options if it looks as if he or she may hold it against you.

You can control, to a large extent, how your getting married is perceived. If you handle it as a matter-of-fact occurrence and you show, from the start, that your performance on the job is not affected by your marriage, then it should pose no career problems. If you know that to advance in your firm, you have to be willing to relocate, you might want to tell your boss at the time of your marriage that you and your husband have discussed the possibility of relocation and he is open to it.

Money and Marriage

Let's talk a little about money (for detailed money management ideas for the career woman, see Chapter Seven on understanding money). In the context of marriage, money can be a source of shared joy or shared conflict, depending on how both partners deal with it. Managing two incomes can be complex and can become an emotionally charged issue unless the two of you sit down and talk about how the money should be managed. You've got lots of options. The basic principle is that both of you should know where the money is going and agree to how the monetary pie is being divided.

Some of the married women we spoke to keep checking accounts separate from their husbands; others have joint accounts. In some relationships, the man keeps the records and pays the bills; in others, the woman does. On that score, we found that people delegate that duty to whoever in the pair is better at it.

The point to remember is that money is power, and unless it is clearly defined, it can be a lethal weapon in a marriage.

As difficult as it may be to manage joint incomes, the most difficult problem already being faced by career women today—and one that will probably increase as women in business earn bigger salaries—is earning more money than their spouses, so much more that they really support the household. There is no easy way to deal with this. Culturally it's still an oddity, and many people will view your spouse as "weak" or "unsuccessful" in some way if he is not the primary breadwinner. Of course, you shouldn't run around discussing salaries anyway, but there are some situations in which your title and position make it so clear that you're the primary breadwinner that actual figures need never be discussed for people to know who is the primary source of income.

How do you deal with this problem? Understanding begins at home. If you and your mate are clear on what your making more money means—and doesn't mean—then, no matter what others may say, you'll survive. If he has any ambivalent feelings—and he may, because culturally he's been taught that he ought to be the breadwinner—get them on the table immediately. Talk them through. Assure him that you don't view him as less of a man because he makes less money.

If he manages the money, he should continue to do so since it is your joint money. If you don't trust him enough to manage the money, you shouldn't be married to him. You can control a lot of how he may feel by your attitude. If you flaunt your bigger salary or decide you have more than 50 percent of the vote on what you do with your money since you earn more of it, then you will have turned money into a weapon, and it can destroy your marriage.

That problem aside, when managing joint incomes, you'll have to take your individual spending and savings habits into account, reaching a compromise you both can live with. When you were living alone, you may have felt comfortable buying a designer suit for $500 and eating peanut butter and jelly for a couple of weeks to compensate for shooting your budget. In a marriage, unless finances are totally separate, a major purchase should be discussed, along with its consequences to your standard of living. It's just not fair to spring that on someone without discussing it in advance. Chapter Seven will give more detailed advice on how to understand and enjoy your money.

Day-to-Day Battle Zones

The routine details of life can sometimes put a strain on a marriage unless you organize and manage them. Approach day-to-day chores with an MBO—a Management by Objectives Plan for getting things done in order of their priority. List what you want to do on an ongoing basis, and decide who will do it. If housework suits neither of you, make the decision to hire someone to do it for you, even if it means eating one less meal out each week. It's just not worth fighting over.

If you want to handle those tasks yourselves, organize and assign them. Try to do this as infrequently as possible, with each of you understanding clearly what's expected, for example, when and how often things like the laundry and the cleaning should be done. If your original plan doesn't work, talk about it, and figure out why—you may decide to redistribute the tasks. If you don't control the routine aspects of your life, they will control you. If the clothes aren't taken to the cleaner's, there will come a morning when you've got a big meeting and nothing suitable to wear. If the laundry isn't done, eventually there will be no sheets and towels. All these things are mundane but necessary, and you want them available to you when you need them.

Some people find it easier to set aside a certain day to do chores; others fit them in as they have an hour or two. This is basically an issue of personal style. Work it the way it's comfortable for you and your mate.

Avoiding a Power Struggle

Mundane chores aren't the only things that can create friction in a relationship. If you compete with each other, your lives together will be a daily battle.

He makes more money than you do, or vice versa. You have a corner office and he doesn't, or vice versa. He manages thirty people, you manage only two, or vice versa. As a writer you have a by-line that's your maiden name, not your married name, and people tend to call him Mr. your name. He sits on five boards of five corporations, you sit on none, or vice versa.

It's all about power, prestige, money and whether or not you're competitive about it with your mate. If you play the power game with each other, you both lose.

Someone once asked novelist-philosopher Ayn Rand whether she thought she was perfect. She answered that she never thought of herself in those terms, that she didn't compare herself to anyone else. She measured her actions and achievements by her own moral code and standards. And that's the whole secret. Truly successful people compete with themselves, not with others. Competing against someone, instead of for and with yourself, is destructive. And nothing kills love and romance faster than one-upmanship.

What does it really matter who makes more money or has a bigger office or staff or a name that's better known? Those things become issues only when they're used in manipulative ways.

Of course, sensitivity is important here. If your professional name is different from your married name and you and your mate are attending a business function for your company, where the natural assumption would be that your names are the same, it's the nice and kind thing to do to introduce your husband as "My husband, Joe Jones." Of course, he would do the same for you.

People tend to forget the importance of manners, of etiquette, yet these rules of social behavior were set down to let people interact in a civilized, thoughtful, and caring manner. Cynics say that familiarity breeds contempt. But we say the key to a successful relationship is to treat each other with the same regard as you would treat a stranger or an important business contact. Using status as a weapon is not only unfair, but bad manners, and it's showing the height of insensitivity to your mate.

Who's Wearing the Pants?

The feminists have brought a lot of sexist thinking to the attention of the American public. Examples abound. Here are a couple: A man who goes after what he wants is assertive; a woman who goes after what she wants is aggressive. A man who has the final word is strong, decisive; a woman who has the final word is a ball-buster, a castrating (expletive deleted). It's sad enough for men and women that women are sometimes subjected to this kind of thinking at work or at large. But it's the pits if that kind of argument is used against you in your own home.

People's sexual identity is central to their identity as individuals. If someone attacks you as not being feminine, that's attacking you at the core. If the man in your life ever stoops to that kind of argument, it's one of the few times not to be flexible. Be firm, and rule those kinds of comments off limits in a discussion about other things. If your femininity (or his suggestion that you lack it) is the topic of conversation, question him carefully. You need to know what he really thinks is feminine and masculine. If he's confused or ambivalent, talk about it. After all, we all grew up in the same culture, in which sexual roles were rigidly defined. He may know in his head that it's all right for a woman to be assertive, but somewhere deep inside him it doesn't "feel" right. Talking about it will help him vent his feelings and clarify his thinking.

A woman can use sexist thinking on her husband as well. On one level, she loves it that he does all the cooking, but on another level, she doesn't think it's manly. Those ambivalent feelings need to be aired, too.

If the man in your life constantly attacks your femininity, even after you've talked about it, you need to identify it as his problem, which he'll have to solve, either by himself or with your help or the help of a counselor. But attacking the sexual identity of your mate is literally and figuratively hitting below the belt and should be ruled off limits.

Rewriting the Marriage Vows: Love, Honor, and Relocate?

You'll follow him anywhere, but does it really mean Detroit? He swore he'd pursue you to the ends of the earth, but will he really have to go to Wahoo, Nebraska?

Ten years ago these questions would never have come up. But

today, as there are more and more dual-career couples, joint job relocation is becoming an issue to deal with, not only for the couples involved but for the companies which employ them. In the March 28, 1979, issue of *Women's Wear Daily*, Samuel Feinberg addressed the problem in his "From Where I Sit" column:

> More and more, the husband in a two-career family is saying to the company that wants to relocate him: "Before I accept the move, you've got to help find my wife a job at least at the level she has reached." Increasingly, although still moderately, it's the working wife who is being transferred and who asks her employer's aid in finding her husband a job in the new location.

Feinberg attributes this information to George H. Rathman, president and chief administrative officer of Merrill Lynch Relocation Management. He quotes Rathman as saying, "One of the most serious problems is that of the household where reliance on a second income is a critical issue. In today's society, women are rising to increasingly meaningful jobs and may find comparable employment elsewhere difficult to obtain. . . .

"The wife is the one being transferred in about 5 percent of the cases, but this percentage is going up. . . . Whether it's the husband or wife who is being moved, our [corporate] clients tend to be more generous in helping the spouse find another job."

Increasingly firms are springing up around the country to deal with relocation, whether it's for individual or group moves, in which an entire business may move from one city to another.

In a dual-career relationship, relocation can be a very tricky business.

In chapter one, we talked about what we would do if Charlie or Peter were offered a job in another city or state or even another country since we all work for multinational companies.

Neither one of us had a pat answer, but by talking it out, we decided we'd have to weigh the career advantage to them versus the disadvantage to us. We'd have to discuss the whole situation as couples, balance all the factors, and then decide. We decided that if the career move represented a major, long-term step up the corporate ladder, we would probably relocate even if we couldn't get the optimum job in the new market. But we'd also want an agreement of reciprocity from our mates for any future moves we might want to make.

In the last year Joyce has been offered several jobs in other states but has made the decision to stay in New York since Peter is here and his future, at least in the long short term, is here. She found she didn't even hesitate. On the other hand, her dream job wasn't offered, either, so maybe it wasn't a fair test.

She knew one couple who had been seemingly happily married for several years; they had combined their family of children from previous marriages, and both worked for the same newspaper. The marriage came apart overnight when he was offered a terrific job in a distant city and decided to take it. She—we'll call her Laurie—was dumbfounded at first that his job was more important to him than she was until she really thought about it herself and realized her job was more important to her than he was. It was an instant eye-opener for both of them.

If you're in a marriage that really works, we think the deciding factor is that jobs come and go, but people last a lifetime.

And it's a lesson for all of us on how important it is to have our priorities straight. If these issues are discussed beforehand, the trauma that occurs at the time could have been avoided or lessened.

Joyce knew another couple for whom relocation worked beautifully. She was an editor, and he was an artist. They lived in New York until she received a fabulous offer from a middlewestern newspaper. They discussed it and decided she should take it. Fortunately for both of them he could do his painting anywhere, so neither their careers nor their marriage suffered.

On the other hand, when a company makes you an offer that involves relocation, and you'd like to explore it, ask whether it would help your husband find a job in its area. More and more, companies are willing to do this, and the best time to ask is when they want you and will try to offer every possible inducement.

On a practical note, unless you request the relocation, you

should expect the company to pay your relocation costs, including moving expenses and some kind of allowance that covers items such as new drapes (the old ones rarely fit), carpeting, or wallpaper that you'll have to leave behind and replace, etc. You should carefully check real estate values and the going rates on apartments; you may need to ask for a cost-of-living adjustment if you're moving from a less expensive to a more expensive area. And if you're relocating to a city you've never seen, ask for a company-paid-for trip for you and your spouse. Try to stay at least for a week to get some feel for the new community. If you have to sell a house and buy a new one, that takes time. Where will you live in the interim? At whose expense? These fringe benefits, trendily called perks, can add up to a lot of money. Find out what the company is willing to do.

If the company is not willing to do most or all of the above, think twice about accepting its offer. It's asking you to uproot your life, the life of your spouse, and, if you have children, their lives, to work for it. What is it willing to do to make that move as easy as possible for you?

Job relocation is a fact of life for many career women, and it's becoming more and more commonplace as women move into the mainstream of corporate jobs. Making the decision to relocate is complex and becomes more complicated if there are a husband and children to consider in the move. We've put together a quiz on how to decide whether you should relocate. The quiz is divided into two major parts: the professional factors to consider when you think about relocating and the personal factors. The personal section is further subdivided, into singles, marrieds, and those with children. Answer yes or no to the questions which apply to you.

Deciding Whether to Relocate

	Yes	No
I. SHOULD WE GO?: *Professional considerations*		
1. The job is a clear promotion.	___	___
2. The direction is in the career path I've chosen.	___	___

	Yes	No
3. I have turned down previous relocation promotions, and I feel that if I turn down this one, I may as well start looking for another job.	___	___
4. The city I've been asked to move to is one that interests me.	___	___
5. I feel unchallenged in my present job, and if I turn down this relocation, I am likely to remain where I am for a period of time.	___	___
6. The increase in salary being offered is in line with the responsibilities of the new job.	___	___
7. My company has agreed to pay all the relocation costs. (See the checklist on how to relocate, which follows this quiz, for a breakdown of relocation costs.)	___	___
8. My husband's career will not suffer any major disruptions if I accept this move.	___	___
9. I really want to go. My feelings are all positive.	___	___

If you've answered yes to six or more of the above nine questions, it looks as if, professionally at least, you should make the move.

II.   SHOULD WE GO?: *Personal considerations*

From a personal standpoint, whether or not you accept a relocation offer depends on what's happening in your life and what's important to you. You need to reevaluate personal priorities, to decide whether the job relocation fits into your life plan. We've divided this section of the quiz into three categories: if you're single; if you have children; if you're married, with no children.

A.   IF YOU'RE SINGLE

	Yes	No
1. I have single friends in the city to which I've been asked to relocate, and they love it there.	___	___

	Yes	No
2. I don't have any friends in the new city, but I've contacted the local newspaper, Chamber of Commerce, and various organizations, and I've received positive reports on the lifestyle.	——	——
3. I am not involved in a serious relationship in my present city, so I'm not leaving behind the man that I love.	——	——
4. There is a thriving singles population in my new city; it's not just a couples' town.	——	——
5. I'm an extrovert who makes friends easily.	——	——
6. I've done some research, and I've found that I can pursue most of my hobbies and interests in my new city (e.g., tennis and other recreational sports, theater, dance, music, etc.).	——	——
7. I adapt easily to change—in fact, I like it.	——	——
8. I'm excited about the adventure of living in a new place, meeting new people, etc.	——	——
9. I can maintain my standard of living or enjoy a higher one in my new city.	——	——
10. I am not running away from anyone or anything by relocating.	——	——

Count your yes answers. If you've answered yes to five or more of the above questions, pack your bags, and follow your career. If the majority of your answers are no's, this is probably not the best time in your personal life to relocate.

B. IF YOU'RE SINGLE OR MARRIED WITH CHILDREN

	Yes	No
1. I have friends in my new city who can help me (or us) adjust in our new situation.	——	——
2. My children are well adjusted, and while they may not be excited at the prospect of moving, they're open to it, and if I'm positive about it, they'll get into the spirit of things.	——	——

	Yes	No

3. My children are young enough so that changing school districts and leaving friends won't be a major problem.

4. I've thoroughly researched the schools in my new city, and I've found that my children will get an education there as good as or better than they will in my present city.

5. My family, especially me, adapts easily to change.

6. The new city seems to have its share of women rearing children alone (if you're single, this applies), and I should be able to find lots of women to relate to.

7. The children will benefit from the change in lifestyle.

8. I've investigated child care resources, and I know I'll be able to find the right person or facility to care for my children while I work.

9. My increased income plus the lower cost of living in my new city will boost our standard of living.

10. I am not running away from anyone or anything.

Count your yes answers. If you have six or more, the move is right for you and your children. If the majority of your answers are noes, relocation is probably not the best decision for you and your family.

C.   IF YOU'RE MARRIED, WITH NO CHILDREN

	Yes	No

1. My husband is totally supportive of my career and has said in the past that he would be willing to move if it meant a major step ahead for me.

	Yes	No
2. I have discussed thoroughly with my husband the opportunity presented by this relocation.	___	___
3. My husband agrees with me that this is a major step up and meets the career goals I've established for myself.	___	___
4. His career is flexible enough (or he is in business for himself and can move the business to the new city) that he'll be able to pursue his career goals in the new city.	___	___
5. We've researched the job possibilities for him, and there is a job offer (or company transfer) he can take that would advance his career or at least maintain his current status.	___	___
6. The new city offers lifestyle advantages for both of us, from recreational facilities to cultural events and interesting people.	___	___
7. My husband feels perfectly comfortable in relocating for my career and knows I would do the same for him.	___	___
8. Our standard of living will remain the same or get better as the result of our move.	___	___

Count the number of yes answers. If you have four or more, the move sounds right for both of you. If you have fewer than four, probably this isn't the best time to move, in terms of your marriage and the best interests of both your careers.

Once you've decided whether to relocate, you'll want to negotiate the best possible terms for relocation. Deal through strength whenever you can. If you've requested the transfer, your position will not be as strong for negotiating money and perks. But if your present company, or a new company, really wants you, make sure you ask for everything you think you'll need to make the relocation as pleasant as possible. And make sure you don't lose any money in the deal. We've put together a checklist of points to consider when negotiating a relocation. Read these carefully, and refer to them whenever you are asked to relocate.

Pragmatic Questions to Ask and Negotiable Items to Ask for Prior to Agreeing to a Job Relocation

Many companies have a firm relocation policy, and your first request should be to see that policy, prior to making a final commitment to relocate.

Depending on whether you're dealing through strength (the company desperately wants you) or weakness (you've requested the transfer), you may be able to negotiate a better deal.

ASK QUESTIONS ABOUT:

1. How much time will you (and your husband or family, if you have one) be given to visit the new city and look for a place to live? The company should pay expenses such as transportation, hotel or motel fees, meals, and incidentals.

The *minimum acceptable response* is a week.

2. Who pays real estate agency fees and any other housing costs?

The *minimum acceptable response* will depend on the tightness of the housing market and whether you are renting or buying a home. In rental situations, the *renter* traditionally pays the fee, and in a tight housing market, you should ask the company to pay this fee because an agency will help you find a place much sooner and will save a lot of your time and effort.

In a buying situation, generally the *seller* pays a commission to the real estate agent, so that you won't have a fee on that end. However, if you own a home in your present community, you should either request that your firm buy your home from you outright and then sell it itself (some companies do this) or at least negotiate that it pay the real estate agency's commission. In addition, you'll need some legal advice about the closing costs and who pays them. If mortgage rates have risen significantly, you need to ask your company whether it will compensate you for the difference between the mortgage rates on your old home and the ones you'll have to pay for your new home. If mortgages are difficult to get in your new city, can the company help in some way?

3. What about payment for incidentals, such as drapes, carpeting, etc. that may have to be replaced in the move from one home to another?

The minimum acceptable response: Some companies have a set allowance for this; other companies will negotiate an amount, but the point is these incidentals can add up to a lot of money, and you shouldn't have to pay those fees if a company has asked you to relocate. You shouldn't make any windfall profits from your move, but you shouldn't find yourself financially in the hole as a result of a move either.

4. Suppose you find a wonderful place to live, but your furniture will not arrive for a month, or the lease can't begin for a period of time, or the closing will not take place for a month. You need to negotiate temporary living expenses for you and your family.

The minimum acceptable response: Depending on the geographical distance of your new location, the timing of the arrival of your furniture, and the time when you can assume a lease or move into a new home (all of which can be documented), the company should pay for your full time in a hotel, with meals and any transportation costs over and above what it would normally cost you to commute. The company should be willing to pay these expenses for at least two weeks and longer if the relocation is cross-country.

5. Now you're ready to make the *actual* move. How much time should you ask for to get settled in?

The *minimum acceptable response* is two days. You should not be expected to carry out your full responsibilities at work and move at the same time. You should gauge the amount of time you need by your own personal priorities.

6. Of course, your company will pay all moving expenses if it asks you to relocate. But what should you expect?

Minimum acceptable response: Moving costs should include a reputable, reliable firm to pack as well as to move all your possessions. Packing takes time and is hard work—your company should be willing to pay to have someone else do this for you. It should also be willing to insure all your possessions against damage or breakage, with the provision that it will either pay the replacement cost or pay repair costs for any damaged items.

7. There could be a problem with my husband finding a job in my new city. What assistance is my company willing to supply?

Minimum acceptable response: It should offer the services of its personnel department and possibly offer that one of its most senior executives, who has connections in your husband's field, will put out feelers for him. Most companies aren't prepared to do more than that. But if you're dealing through a position of great strength, you can ask for more help in finding your husband a job. All the firm can say is no.

8. What about the taxes I will be responsible for paying for relocation expenses paid for by my company? The Internal Revenue Service categorizes these expenses as income.

Minimum acceptable response: Before you negotiate this item, see a good tax accountant to find out how the IRS is likely to deal with these expenses and how much it will cost you in actual tax dollars. Then negotiate with your company for a salary boost to compensate for the tax bite.

9. What happens if you relocate and suddenly there is a major reorganization, or the company gets sold, or your boss gets fired, and you find yourself without a job in a strange city?

Minimum acceptable response: Discuss this issue *before* agreeing to relocate. Most companies will deny that this kind of situation will ever occur, but you should cover it and ask for some kind of written commitment as to what would happen to you if there were some major change in the company within one year of relocation and your services were no longer needed. The best item to negotiate—especially if your company is taking you out of an area where you could find a job in your field easily and is moving you to an area where you can't—is to request that it relocate you back—with the same benefits—to your original city. If it refuses to do this, at least try to negotiate a six-month guarantee of position.

These guidelines should serve you well in any *domestic* (within the United States) relocation. But what happens when you work for a multinational company that wants to send you to another country? The following guidelines will help you negotiate the best deal in international relocations.

Relocating Internationally

Review the points in the guidelines for domestic relocation. Many of them apply as well to international relocation. Additionally, look at these factors:

1. Will your company pay for a private school for your children in your new country if the language is different from your own? Or will it pay transportation costs back and forth if your children are in boarding school or college in the States?
2. Are chauffeurs normal or necessary in your new country? Will the company pay for one?
3. What about currency protection to ensure your salary and standard of living in your new country?
4. What about an international living allowance? Many companies give you 10 percent of your salary as a bonus for leaving the country on their behalf.
5. Will the company pay for a tax service to file the complicated returns you'll have to make as a foreign national? A word of

advice: Get your own accountant to review the work of the company-hired accountant to make sure you are getting all your deductions. This will cost you some money now but could save you a lot later.

6. Is there a cost-of-living allowance in countries where it is more expensive to live?
7. Is there a housing subsidy in countries where housing is more expensive than it is in the United States? Japan and the Middle East fit into this category.
8. Is there a car allowance?
9. Will the company provide language lessons for you and your family?
10. Will the company provide home leave, all expenses paid (one trip a year to your home country)?
11. Will your company provide for rest and relaxation trips for you and your family if you're assigned to a "hardship" country (some Middle Eastern countries, among others, fit into this category)?
12. Will your company provide full medical coverage in your new country? This is standard, so make sure you get it.
13. A company is obligated to relocate you back to your home country should you quit or get fired. Get this commitment in writing if there is no written policy to cover it.
14. How long a commitment must you make for staying in your new country?

Of course, all the provisions you wanted guaranteed for a domestic relocation, such as moving insurance, interim housing costs, etc., should be negotiated in an international relocation.

The Long-Distance Commuter

Some dual-career couples have come up with a unique way to solve the relocation problem. Right up front we'll say it's fraught with potential problems and is not for everyone. These couples commute, from one city to another, even from one state to another. Depending on the distances involved and the cost of commuting, they may see each other every weekend, or once a month, or once every couple of months. The longer the periods of separation, obviously, the more difficult a life it is to lead.

In most cases, even if you see each other every week, you need to maintain two households and probably two cars, unless one or both of you is in an urban center with good public transportation. Your day-to-day sharing will be done by telephone or not at all. When Joyce was in Akron, her phone bills to Peter in New York were monumental. All those kinds of expenses need to be realistically budgeted.

Forget about what you've come to know as a normal social life. If you commute, you are neither attached nor single. You're just different. It makes socializing tough, especially for the one going to the new city or town who has to make new friends.

One couple we know commutes weekly between two cities in the South. It's a short, inexpensive plane ride, and the last time we spoke with them, their two-year-old marriage was holding up well. Both said they wouldn't want to do this forever, but they could maintain their separate lives, coming together weekends, for another year or two.

Another couple we know has a very different story. Terry is the editor in chief of a major newspaper. Her husband has worked in publishing and is now a computer programmer. They've been married for twelve years and have commuted for seven, over very long distances—a couple of thousand miles, in fact. Long-distance commuting has worked for them although Terry says she knows it's certainly different and could work only for two people who need a lot of time on their own.

"We're both more committed to other things than we are to each other, and we know it," she says. "We also like a different lifestyle. Carl loves the country, hates cities. I'm the opposite. We really couldn't live together.

"When we're apart, we lead separate lives, with separate friends and sometimes romantic relationships. The people we become involved with know that we're married and that in the end Carl and I will be together.

"We got married in the sixties, and we both were very different people then, much more conventional. If we met today, we probably wouldn't marry. On the other hand, if I had to marry someone, I'm so glad it was Carl, because we can handle our marriage this way.

"We both have this mental image of ourselves thirty or forty years from now, sitting and rocking on the porch of our little house in the country, swapping stories about what we've done with our lives."

Commuting is an option. Probably not for everyone, but certainly a solution for some, and new situation problems call for innovative, imaginative solutions. And lots of flexibility.

When You Live with Your Mate ... and Work with Him

"Could you work with your husband?" we asked the women we interviewed. Most of them said no.

Sandra said yes. Both she and her husband are recruiters, currently working for different companies. But their dream is to work together. They feel they complement each other, professionally as well as personally—each places people in different industries and has different strengths.

Joyce and Peter worked together for five years, he in advertising and she as an editor, and really enjoyed it. They could bounce ideas off each other, work as a team to get a job done, communicate in half sentences because they were so closely attuned. They could also fight about the work without carrying it over into their personal lives.

Many small—and some large—businesses are run by husband-and-wife teams and passed along from one generation to another: the classic mom-and-pop operation. Many creative couples can work as a team—Ruth Gordon and Garson Kanin come to mind.

Joyce has known newspaper couples who literally worked side by side all day, and their marriages not only lasted but prospered.

If you work together, it's probably more important to shift gears at the end of the day since it would be so easy to just continue work and work-related conversation while you're at home. You have the same community of interest, know the same cast of characters. It's easy, but it's not beneficial to the personal side of the relationship. Work and play are different, they serve different purposes, and it's best to keep them separate.

If you own your own business together, the overlap between work and free time will be tremendous. Especially at the start of a new business, you'll work long hours and be totally caught up in what you're doing. If you and your husband or mate are really a team, really know, understand, respect, and love each other, starting and working in your own business can be a tremendous adventure. You are truly equal partners, dealing through strength, to achieve short- and long-term goals. You may need more time to be alone, away from each other, just because you work long, hard hours side by side. But your times together can be even more rewarding because of the common goals in your personal and business lives.

There seems to be a return to husband-and-wife business teams as younger people leave the large urban areas to try their luck, on their own, in a private enterprise. One young couple who publish a weekly newspaper in northern California had the culmination of their journalists' dream last year when they won a Pulitzer Prize for their investigative report on Synanon, the drug rehabilitation center based in California. The two are now collaborating on a book on their experiences.

Sharing that kind of adventure and professional success can bring you closer together, give your lives more meaning on a whole other level. But it's not for everyone. First of all, not everyone wants to start his or her own business. Secondly, in terms of interests or temperaments, a husband and wife may not be suited to working together, and they wouldn't find it an enjoyable experience.

If you work together in the same corporation, that presents other obstacles—and pleasures. There are still a number of companies that won't hire a husband-and-wife team—they'll tell you they don't like nepotism, which isn't the issue. Nepotism means hiring and promoting someone because he or she is a member of your family and you own the company. Hiring a husband-and-wife team does not fit that definition. Nevertheless, some companies have that policy and may even enforce it after the fact, so that one of you will be asked to resign.

If it's okay with the corporation, you have to decide whether it's okay with you. Many people meet on the job, and if they fall in love and get married, they just go on from there. The advantage to that is that they were known first by their superiors and co-workers as separate individuals. In that case, the fact that they marry will probably be seen as incidental.

If you come into a company as a husband-and-wife team, there may be more difficulties. For one thing, you may be evaluated as a package because you're a couple. If there is a relocation possibility for one of you but not the other, the company will probably not even make you the offer. If getting promoted is dependent on relocation, you may sit in the same position unless one or both of you go elsewhere.

One trap that most companies avoid as a matter of policy is to have one spouse report to the other. How can you objectively evaluate the work performance of the person you love? Even if you can do it and are totally fair, who will ever believe you? If your company doesn't have a policy against this tactic, avoid it on your own. It's a no-win situation.

If there's any element of competitiveness in your marriage, you may want to think carefully about working for the same company. What if one of you gets promoted and the other one doesn't? Or one of you goes to the big sales meeting and the other one doesn't get an invitation?

If you get an offer to work together for the same company, evaluate the offer not only from an individual career standpoint but form the standpoint of what is good for your marriage.

Surviving Crises . . . Together

Even in the best-planned lives, crises can occur. In a marriage, it can be a mutual crisis—the marriage itself is in trouble; a child is seriously ill; there is a financial problem—or it can be an individual crisis—one of you is fired or ill; your business or his goes bankrupt; whatever. These traumatic events can make or break a relationship. It really depends on how they're handled.

Love, caring, understanding, and support go a long way. You give love and get love. Crises vary in degree. What may not seem so serious to you may be crucially important to your husband. That's where sensitivity to his needs enters the picture. If each of you is in the midst of your own individual crisis, you'll need to be that much more sensitive to each other. It's doubly difficult to be tuned into someone else's pain if you're in pain yourself.

The crucial point to remember is that you need to be there for the person you love. You need to help *at the time.*

A woman we know whose marriage ended in divorce said she left her husband because "He was just never *there* for me. When I was going through a terrible time with my son from a previous marriage, he not only gave me no support but complained that our domestic problems were interfering with *his* work. He wanted to stay married but get a place of his own where he could work in peace. He has one now, but he lost me."

You pay to play. You share in each other's successes and in your defeats or temporary setbacks. You grow together, survive together, and come through it stronger and closer to one another.

With love, the more you give away, the more you get back.

A marriage or romantic relationship can be the most rewarding experience you will have in your life. It can be more lasting than any job, even supersede a career. Emotionally it can be a major source of fuel and support from which you will reap benefits for the rest of your life.

But like any long-term, complex goal, it takes careful choosing at the start; time, effort, and caring throughout; and flexibility. Once you have achieved a relationship of two, you may decide you want to add to your family by having children. For career women, that can be a complex choice although more and more career women are choosing to become mothers. With a healthy, happy marriage as a base, you're ready to consider your next option—having children or not—in Chapter Five.

FIVE

WHEN YOU HAVE CHILDREN

Nothing in my life has been as rewarding to me as having children. I love my two boys so much. And my husband and I seem closer somehow because of the feelings we share in raising the boys. I think I'm a good mother—loving, caring, interested in what my children do. And my husband is a terrific father. He really loves being with the boys. We both look forward to our time together as a family. We work at being a close family unit. I waited until both my boys were in school before going back to work as a management consultant, and my hours are flexible enough so that I never miss important events in their lives. For us, parenthood has been a tremendous experience in the giving and getting of love—the best kind of sharing.

My daughter is the most important person in my life. She was totally my choice. I had her when I was thirty because I knew I wouldn't be young forever. I consciously decided not to have children in my twenties because I wasn't prepared to raise a child—I knew I couldn't be grown-up, unselfish. And I wanted a child to love, so I wanted to be ready when I finally did get pregnant. When I had my daughter, I was able to spend all my time with her when she was a baby because I wasn't working. Even now I prefer to work at home, writing, so that I can be there for her. I think that's very important.

Here I am, pregnant with my first child at thirty-five. We decided to have a child just a few months ago, when I realized my safe childbearing time was running out—at least to have a first child. The baby will cause a lot of changes in our lives that will be difficult since Bob already has three children to support from his first marriage. But it's something we want to do, and we're very happy about it. I'll take some time off—a month or two—then go back to work. Since I own my own business, my schedule can be flexible enough so that I can spend time with our baby and still do my job.

THERE HAVE BEEN a number of books written about working mothers. They contain a lot of helpful information and advice, but working mothers and career mothers are different. Working is a much broader term, covering everything from a part-time job to a job that may be satisfying but is done in a set number of hours—say, from nine to five each day—and when you leave the office, you leave the work behind. Career implies a long-term focus on the work you choose to do. It implies commitment, longer hours, more responsibility, special credentials and skills. And when a woman has a career, the work she does is acknowledged—by her, her family, and her employer—as a top priority in her life.

We've devoted a chapter to children because for the career woman, having children is the one exception to many of the principles in this book. Children are a large part of having it all for many career women, but they also limit options in other areas. The trade-off is love: the love you have for your children and the love you receive from them.

In this chapter we'll deal with the joys and problems of having children. We'll talk about the logistics of when and how to have them, how to fit children into your career plan, how to choose day care and other support systems, how to manage your time so that you enjoy your career and your family. We've talked to the best experts we know—career women who have children—to gather the advice we'll share with you. Because having children is a life decision, even though it may not apply to you today, it could very well apply to you tomorrow. Since women have the biological capability to become mothers, having children is always a conscious choice. We've tried to discuss all the points to be considered, so if and when you decide to become a mother, you'll have the benefit of the wisdom of those who have gone before you.

To Have or Have Not

The decision to have children is a pivotal one for a career woman for a couple of reasons. For one thing, children are totally demanding—totally dependent on you for the first few years and largely dependent on you until they reach adulthood. You and your husband (if you are married) will have to meet their needs and demands. And sometimes you'll have to meet them at the expense of a part of the existing framework of your lives. Some women give up their careers to have children. Others leave their jobs for a period of time, from a couple of weeks to a couple of years. Still others change their work schedules or the kind of work they do to accommodate children. Some men are beginning to change their schedules and hours in order to share parenting although this trend is just beginning and certainly isn't yet the norm. In book after book on working mothers, what they most often give up to have children and a job (let alone a career) is leisure time. Children are simply a part of the juggling act done by all career women that takes more time, more effort, and more careful planning and organization.

Children are the one irrevocable decision you make. You can end a bad relationship, leave a marriage that doesn't work, resign from a job that's unsatisfying, even shift careers to gain more fulfillment. But once you have children, they are an immutable fact of your life. You can't walk away, and your responsibility becomes total.

The decision to have a child should never be hasty. If you're going to be a career mother, the decision needs even more thought and planning so that you can continue your career and bring up a family at the same time. It also takes the full agreement of both partners in a marriage because juggling a career and a child takes the cooperation, help, and understanding of both parents. If you have any illusions that you can be Superwoman and rear a child single-handedly while pursuing a career, forget it. Women who are widowed or divorced and even those who have consciously decided to become parents while single will tell you that they need help—some kind of support system—to do both. They either pay for help or rely on extended families to ensure quality care for their child or children while they pursue careers.

In some ways, you share the problems of all working mothers—the need for part-time or full-time help or adequate day care facilities; the shifting of gears necessary to change your focus from work to children to husband every day; the planning ahead of the details of life to make it all work smoothly. But in some ways your juggling act is easier because your financial reserves and economic potential may be greater than those of a clerical or pink-collar worker. On the other hand, your hours may be longer, and you may have business travel or weekend work commitments that make the scheduling of time with your family more difficult.

You need to weigh the value and benefits of having children against what you feel is most important in your life. In order to evaluate the decision as objectively as possible, one of the most difficult images you must confront is that of the woman who needs to "fulfill her biological destiny." You may think that this old myth has not influenced you at all, but think about it again since it has been a powerful bromide in our culture and may have affected your feelings on a subconscious level.

Try to talk to a number of women who have had children. Talk to both career women and women who have stayed at home until their children were of school age or beyond. Go on your own fact-finding mission, and talk to the people with expertise in this field—mothers. It's important to talk to a number of women, with varied feelings and situations, so that you don't get only one view— whether it's very negative or very positive.

If you were reared as an only child and have no experience being around children, give yourself and your mate a tryout at being parents. Many couples will be only too happy to let you take care of their children for a day, an evening, or a weekend. Ask to "borrow" the child of a friend, and spend some time with her or him. Plan some activities—a trip to the zoo or amusement park, a museum or day trip for an older child. If you can, have the child spend at least one night with you. Experience how it feels to take care of the needs of a child on a day-to-day basis. Get to know and be with children of different ages. Mothers will tell you that even with their own children, they preferred some ages to others. One woman we know really loved infants; another said that the infancy of her child was a boring time for her because she got no response from her daughter. She preferred the ages of three on. Toddlers are one experience; preschoolers, another; seven- to eight-year-olds, something else again; and adolescents, almost a world unto themselves. Experience as many of these stages as you can.

You owe it to yourself, your husband, and any children you

may bring into the world to be as sure as possible that not only is having children what you want, but that you want children enough to change your lifestyle, and happily, because of the joy children will bring to your life. Understand, a child is a lifetime commitment.

Sally felt strongly when her son was born that she wanted to be there at the end of the day to bathe him, feed him, and put him to bed. What she failed to take into account was the lifestyle that she and her executive husband, Jack, had developed over the ten years they had been married. And she didn't realize how much of her energy caring for her son would take. She thought that her husband would help and that it would be a wonderful time of family closeness. What happened was different from her expectations.

"All that effort took a terrible toll on my marriage," she says. "I was just too exhausted after a difficult day and caring for the baby at night to pay any attention to Jack at all. And inside, Jack was busy resenting me, and I started to resent him. We just hadn't properly evaluated the consequences of having a child and how it would affect our careers. For one thing, we both were doing a lot of business travel, and it would increase as we grew in our careers. Our responsibilities were greater, too. Was our son really going to suffer if his mother wasn't there every night? We knew that we were in trouble, that something would have to give.

"It took some counseling, which we decided to seek before making the decision to divorce—things were that bad. Counseling helped us find a solution—and it wasn't even that complicated. We decided to get full-time live-in help. I had to discard the mother guilts of not doing everything for my son myself. And Jack had to stop putting me down for not doing all the things traditionally associated with motherhood. Our son was absolutely fine through the whole thing, but I firmly believe he escaped unscathed because we caught it soon enough and both of us refused to live our lives as unhappy people—baby or no baby."

Doreen made another kind of choice. A journalist, when she found she was pregnant, she left it open-ended whether she would return to her newspaper after the birth of her baby.

"After Cindy was born, I decided I just couldn't miss watching her grow and develop. I had worked in my profession for ten years and had accomplished much of what I wanted to accomplish. I decided to take two or three years off to enjoy my child, doing a little free-lance writing just to keep my hand in. Part of what I had to consider in deciding whether to return to work was the irregular hours I had as a working editor. I didn't think that kind of schedule would leave me enough time to enjoy my husband and family, at least not while Cindy was so young."

If you're married and decide to have children, sit down with your husband, and do some very careful, detailed planning in terms of finances, time management, changes in how you live (if you are considering becoming a single adoptive parent, make sure of your finances and support systems before making the final decision). Try to anticipate the best way to get through your pregnancy and the early years of child care. Do you want to work right up to the birth of your child and go back to work a few days or a few weeks after? Do you want to take some time off? If so, how much time? Will you resign from your job or take a leave of absence? If you want to return to work immediately, what kind of help will you need? What will it cost? How do you go about finding it? In large urban areas, where housing can be a problem, you may even have to move into a larger apartment to make room for a child, or you may have to buy a house in the suburbs. Are you willing to do this? Can you afford it?

Finally, don't have children to save a marriage that's faltering. The women we talked to who had children stressed that the best time to have them is when your life is in order. If your marriage is in trouble, children won't save it. More likely, children will make for additional stress in an already shaky situation. And of course, it's grossly unfair to an infant to put the burden of your marriage on his or her newly formed, fragile shoulders.

Single Parenthood

As women have become financially independent, some of them have chosen to become mothers without getting married, through adoption or by becoming pregnant without marrying the father of the child. Single parents can successfully rear one child or several, so if that's your choice, it's an achievable goal. But it is difficult; that means it's even more important to think through all aspects carefully, including how those close to you, from your family to your employer, will view your decision. You will need their understanding and support. Financially you will be assuming a lifetime burden, so make sure you can afford it. Talk to other single parents —men and women—to benefit from their advice and experience. Be aware that should you want to marry at some point in the future, part of the package will include your child or children, and that could limit your options since some men will not want to assume the added burden of a family when all they really want is a wife.

If you become a single parent through divorce or death, your life may change radically, and part of your support system will be gone. Your husband will no longer be there, and you may not be able to count on child support in the case of divorce since many men refuse or neglect to pay it. In the case of a death, your finances may be totally shattered unless there are enough insurance and savings to get you through. You'll lose emotional and often financial support in one blow. You need to develop alternative support systems, through friends, other family members, and groups like Parents Without Partners. Just seeing others coping in the same situation will help, and their experiences and advice can be very beneficial.

You'll also have to deal with any trauma your child or children will suffer. Death or divorce can shatter family life. In the case of divorce, keeping things as amicable as possible with your ex-husband will make it a much easier transition for your children. They need to know that the love of both parents is constant. In the case of death, comfort your child and tell him or her as much as he is able to deal with at the time. A very small child will not fully comprehend the finality of death, and you may have to answer his or her questions in stages. Seek professional help if you need it in coping with the great change going on in your family life.

Fitting a Child into Your Career Plan

The success or failure of many things in life depends on timing. When should you have a child? How should the birth of your child fit into your career plan? If this approach sounds cold and calculating to you, consider the alternative: an unplanned pregnancy, with no thought given to how you'll take care of your child and pursue your career.

Of the women we know who have children, there seem to be two schools of thought on when to have them: Have them young, in your early twenties, before starting your career, or have them later, after you're thirty, when your career is already established. There are pros and cons to both options. Listen to two women who had their children very young.

"I was pregnant at the age of twenty," Sherry told us. "It was a totally unplanned thing. I didn't have the sense or the maturity to understand the responsibilities of what was happening to me. What I did was look around me and figure that millions of women were having children. Obviously I could do it, too. At that point I really envied women who were in control of their lives because at that point I seemed totally out of control."

Looking back at it now, at the age of thirty-five, Sherry admits that everything worked out even though her first pregnancy was unplanned. She has two children, a son, fourteen, and a daughter, eleven, and three stepchildren from her second husband's first marriage. She is also the president of her own company, earning a six-figure income. But in order to build her career and bring up her children, she had to give up a lot of time with them. She says, "I hired a 'wife' to do all the household chores and care for the children. But there were many days when the children were small that I would rather have been at home."

Carrie also had her first child at twenty and planned it that way. She was still in college at the time, editing the school newspaper, and managed to edit right through her pregnancy and after.

"Luckily I could schedule my classes around my husband's work schedule and caring for my son. And Harry, my husband, helped a lot. Luckily for all of us Harry began cooking and really got into it; that was good because I had never been the best cook in the world. He just took over and freed some of my time.

"I worked as a reporter after I finished school, again scheduling my work hours to coordinate with Harry's—he was also a reporter, so we could get complementary shifts. I worked until my daughter was born. After that, I free-lanced from home. Luckily I *could* work at home.

"I'm really happy that I had my children so young—in a way, we grew up together. In your twenties, you have more energy, more of a sense of fun, and more patience. Now that I'm in my thirties, I don't know whether I'd have the same patience and enjoy mothering small children as much as I did then."

Now that both her children are in school, Carrie works full time for a business publication.

Increasingly today women seem to be having children later in life. There are many post-thirty mothers. Bettye, whose daughter, Ashley, is almost three, is one of them.

"I had Ashley when I was thirty-five. It seems a much more settled age, and certainly financially you're more able to afford having children, which is expensive, no matter where you live and raise them. I know I'm more mature now than I was in my twenties. I make decisions much more calmly and rationally now than I did then. And in my case, I have developed more patience over the years than I had when I was younger.

"Although my pregnancy was unplanned, I made a conscious decision to go through with the birth of my child. It was the right time for me, even though my marriage was falling apart, because in other areas I had already done a good many of the things I wanted to do. I had traveled to many places, was established in my career, understood what makes and breaks up relationships. I would never feel now that having a child had cheated me out of any of these things. I already had them. Having a child seemed one of the most wonderful things left to do that I had not done. And I haven't been disappointed. Having Ashley has added a whole new, exciting, loving dimension to my life. And it's one that I was ready to handle."

Once you've decided on the right time for you to have a child or children, how do you fit that into your career plan and, in a wider sense, into the life you want for yourself and your husband? Or if you are a mother at home contemplating beginning or re-starting your career, how does that fit into your plans for child rearing and caring for your family?

We've put together some guidelines to help you decide the best time in your career to become pregnant. Since the advent of the pill, women have had total control over whether and when they became pregnant, and for the career woman, timing can be crucial if she wants to continue her career during her pregnancy and after the birth of her child. Recent state and federal legislation prohibits employers from discriminating against women because of pregnancy, and you should be familiar with your rights and guarantees under this legislation. But legislation aside, some times are better than others to become pregnant. How do you decide when in your career to become pregnant, and how do you proceed with your career while you're pregnant? We think these guidelines will help.

I. PLANNING YOUR PREGNANCY TO COINCIDE WITH YOUR CAREER GOALS

Do these points describe your situation?

1. I have been at my company long enough to have established credibility for myself.
2. My staff situation is such that there will be backup for me during the time I will not be working.
3. There are no major organizational changes planned within the next months in which I will be expected to participate.
4. I feel secure about my standing with my boss, and I don't feel

he/she will have any major difficulties handling the situation if I become pregnant.

5. I have been in my position long enough so that it is organized and running smoothly.

If you can't agree with all five points, it doesn't mean that you shouldn't ever get pregnant, but it is an indication that there may be a better time or, should you decide to go ahead anyway, that there will be some problems. It is not a comfortable situation to find yourself in the midst of a major job change or departmental upheaval when you are two or three months pregnant. It's not that you can't do it, but since you do have the option of deciding when you'll get pregnant, why not choose the best time, when your career is at a certain plateau that can make a working pregancy comfortable?

II. PROCEEDING WITH YOUR CAREER WHILE PREGNANT

You've discovered you're pregnant, and you know the approximate due date. You're excited and happy. What actions do you take now in relation to work?

Rule 1—Stop and Think

Pregnancy is a long process: nine months. You may not want to announce your pregnancy right away. Do you really want to deal with seven months of questions? Each business meeting you walk into will begin with "How are you today, Jane?" "How's the baby?" "Can you feel it kicking yet?" "What are you going to do for child care?" "How long will you be gone from work?" And on and on. Of course, all the questions are well motivated, but do you really want to focus on a personal issue for so long a period of time?

Rule 2—Make a Firm Decision and Stick to It

Either tell everyone from the beginning and live with it, or decide to tell people gradually, on a need-to-know basis. Determine whom you need to tell and when you need to tell them.

Suggested Game Plan

Month Three: Tell your boss. Only. Tell him or her in a matter-of-fact way. Give dates; discuss how long you plan to be gone from work; detail your backup plan for how work will be handled in your absence. If you are due at a slow time of year for your business, mention that point and incorporate it into your backup plan. If you will be gone during your peak business period, give a detailed description of your backup plan. Tell your boss exactly how you will have the job handled on a project-by-project basis, and put it in writing, so he or she has it for handy reference. If you feel you will need extra help in your department while you're gone, make those plans now. Tell your boss whom you want and what you want that person to do. Also, make absolutely sure that your boss understands that he or she is the only person you have chosen to tell at this juncture and that you would like the information held in strictest confidence. Explain your reasons for not telling everyone at once, and let your boss know when you do plan to tell others.

Month Four: Tell your immediate subordinates. Again, make sure that they understand you are telling them in confidence. Outline the plans that have by now been agreed upon by you and your boss for how the department will function in your absence. Talk about the timing and the goal setting for that period. And ask for a little patience from them until the baby is born and you return to work. You will tire more easily during your pregnancy, and your stamina will probably decrease as the months go by. Tell them what to expect, and don't hesitate to be human in front of them. Explain to them that you don't want your pregnancy to become a focal point of office interest, and that you plan to be very low-key about it. Ask for their help and support.

Months Five and Six: People will start to suspect because you're probably putting on weight. The first one who has the nerve to ask either you or one of your subordinates whether you're pregnant should be told. Tell your subordinates when it's okay to answer these questions. The word will spread like wildfire through the office grapevine. Some co-workers will be offended that you didn't tell them, but they'll probably understand when you explain your reasons for telling only your boss and your subordinates.

Now relax. Let the goodwill people take over. You couldn't stop them if you wanted to. Human nature being what it is, people will take a friendly interest in your pregnancy. You will be told a hundred pregnancy stories, so be prepared to be patient. Just continue to act as professionally as possible during meetings and while conducting business. Treat your pregnancy as a condition that really doesn't differentiate you from anyone else in that job.

Months Seven through Nine: You will tire easily. Plan your days carefully to take advantage of the energy you have. Rely more on your staff, and begin putting your backup systems into place, working closely to supervise the implementation of the arrangements you've made to cover for you during your absence. Continue to try not to let your pregnancy become the focal point of any professional meeting or situation. If you don't focus on it, talk about it a lot, and complain, you will find people gradually moving away from the subject.

Work until the last possible moment—listening, of course, to your doctor and your body. Basically, if you are healthy and the baby is fine, there is no reason not to work right up until labor. In the meantime, months seven through nine are the time to plan your child care system. If you are going to hire a housekeeper or nurse, find her now, and have her on board for the day you return from the hospital.

What About Returning to Work?

Speak to your doctor about your own situation. Most doctors recommend about six to eight weeks after a normal birth, but some career women are back at their desks within a few days or a week or two. Listen to your own system. The women we talked to found the faster they returned to work, the better they felt.

When you return to work, review how your backup system worked in your absence. Praise those who did well, have a talk with any who did not, and get about the business of your dual careers—businesswoman and mother.

In addition to the guidelines for when to become pregnant, we've devised a quiz that will give you a strong indication of whether the time is right. Answer the questions honestly, circling the number that corresponds to your answer. Add up your score, and see the key at the end of the quiz to find out what it means.. Bear in mind that this quiz is just another guideline; it's not gospel. If your score says the timing is wrong, but you want a child now, by all means, go ahead.

We've broken down the elements involved in your decision whether to get pregnant into three major categories which affect your career:

I. The company you work for
II. The position you hold within that company
III. The credibility you've established in both the position and the company

PART I: THE COMPANY

1. Other women in my company have worked through a pregnancy and returned to work after the birth of the child.

9	3	7	5
Yes	No	Unsure	Not Applicable

2. Women in my company are generally treated professionally and are well accepted within the executive ranks of the corporation.

9	3	7	5
Yes	No	Unsure	Not Applicable

3. There aren't any precedents in my company for women work-

ing through pregnancy and returning after the birth of the child, but the company is aware of the existing legislation prohibiting job discrimination against pregnant women, and I am reasonably sure it will treat me fairly.

9	3	7	5
Yes	No	Unsure	Not Applicable

4. My company is totally dominated by Old Boy Network males who feel that all wives, especially pregnant ones, should be at home.

3	9	7	5
Yes	No	Unsure	Not Applicable

5. There have been quite a few instances of professional women in the company who elected not to continue working through pregnancy and after the birth of the child.

3	9	7	5
Yes	No	Unsure	Not Applicable

6. My company is part of the fashion industry, and it frowns on any workers who don't look chicly thin. My pregnant appearance would embarrass management.

3	9	7	5
Yes	No	Unsure	Not Applicable

7. Because of the high level of technical or educational expertise required to be hired as a professional within my company, most people pay no attention to such personal things as being pregnant.

9	3	5	7
Yes	No	Unsure	Not Applicable

8. While my company is used to dealing with pregnancies in the

clerical ranks, I would be the first at the management level, and I feel it would just not be accepted.

3	9	7	5
Yes	No	Unsure	Not Applicable

9. I am quite new to the company, and I don't know how it would react to my becoming pregnant.

3	9	7	5
Yes	No	Unsure	Not Applicable

10. I am unhappy with the company and the way it's run, to the extent that I'm thinking of leaving.

3	9	5	7
Yes	No	Unsure	Not Applicable

ADD UP THE TOTAL OF YOUR ANSWERS TO PART I, AND PUT THE NUMBER HERE _____.

PART II. THE POSITION

1. I have established a logical backup system for my department, so that when I tell my boss I'm pregnant, I can outline the system which will be in effect during my absence.

7	3	5
Yes	No	Not Applicable

2. I've been in my position long enough for management to feel confident of my abilities.

7	3	5
Yes	No	Not Applicable

3. I have been waiting a long time for a promotion, and I've been given certain signals that it is imminent.

3	5	7
Yes	No	Not Applicable

4. My boss has just resigned, and it looks as if I may be tapped for the promotion.

<u>   3   </u>   <u>   5   </u>   <u>   7   </u>
  Yes   No   Not Applicable

5. I am unhappy with my position and am considering either asking for a transfer or seeking another position outside my company.

<u>   3   </u>   <u>   7   </u>   <u>   5   </u>
  Yes   No   Not Applicable

6. I have just hired almost a totally new staff (or new assistant), whom I haven't finished training.

<u>   3   </u>   <u>   7   </u>   <u>   5   </u>
  Yes   No   Not Applicable

7. My job is a pressure pot, and although I like my work, the pressure is getting to me a bit lately.

<u>   3   </u>   <u>   7   </u>   <u>   5   </u>
  Yes   No   Not Applicable

8. I have my job under control, and I know management thinks so because of its positive comments on my recent performance evaluation. While it said my future with the company is excellent, it didn't mention any imminent plans to move or promote me.

<u>   7   </u>   <u>   3   </u>   <u>   5   </u>
  Yes   No   Not Applicable

9. Although I love my job, at the moment the demands on my time are quite heavy, and I'm doing a lot of business travel.

<u>   3   </u>   <u>   7   </u>   <u>   5   </u>
  Yes   No   Not Applicable

ADD UP THE TOTAL OF YOUR ANSWERS TO PART II, AND PUT THE NUMBER HERE ____.

PART III.   YOUR CREDIBILITY IN THE COMPANY

1. I am well enough established within my field that I am beginning to build a strong internal reputation and am becoming known in my profession as well.

7	3	5
Yes	No	Not Applicable

2. I've been in my current position for two years, and management is pleased with my performance. My staff performs beautifully.

7	3	5
Yes	No	Not Applicable

3. My superiors regularly turn to me for answers and advice. I have earned the reputation for knowing the answers and following through on promises and commitments.

7	3	5
Yes	No	Not Applicable

4. My boss recently confided in me that I am his designated backup and expressed great confidence in the job I am doing.

7	3	5
Yes	No	Not Applicable

5. I am sufficiently established and well known in my field that search firms are beginning to seek me out as a candidate for opportunities in other corporations.

7	3	0
Yes	No	Not Applicable

6. The promotion I was expecting did not materialize. In fact, the company has brought a new person in as my immediate superior, putting another level between me and top management.

3	7	0
Yes	No	Not Applicable

7. Although it's hard for me to admit, I've been told by my company to "look around" for another position. I am reasonably sure I won't be fired, but I also know I have no future there.

3	7	0
Yes	No	Not Applicable

8. My mentor just got fired.

3	7	5
Yes	No	Not Applicable

9. My mentor was just promoted to a major position.

3	7	5
Yes	No	Not Applicable

10. My company has just selected me to participate in a much-sought-after educational program, generally reserved for those on the way up in my organization.

7	3	0
Yes	No	Not Applicable

ADD UP THE TOTAL OF YOUR ANSWERS TO PART III, AND PUT THE NUMBER HERE ____.

NOW WRITE IN THE TOTAL FROM ALL THREE PARTS ____.

The following key will tell you what your score means:

Totals between 223 and 189: You seem to be very secure within your position and your company; this makes it a good time in your career to become pregnant. Your company may be surprised but will most likely be confident that you'll return to your well-run department or position. Although there may be future changes on your horizon, they don't seem imminent enough to cause any problems.

Totals between 188 and 155: Although this may not be the perfect time to become pregnant, it's not a bad time either. Perhaps there have been some recent changes, or you're feeling a bit unsettled in either your position or your company, but you're not unhappy or unsettled enough to have to worry. Your job is secure, and your company will probably be understanding of your pregnancy. You should make careful plans and watch for any problem areas.

Totals between 154 and 121: You seem sufficiently unsettled at this time that you may want to wait to get pregnant. Of course, as we mentioned in the introduction to our quiz, if all the other elements in your life say that this is the right time to get pregnant, go ahead, but be prepared for some problems in the career area. Go back and read the test to determine where your unsettling factors are surfacing, and see what you can do to fix the problems.

Totals between 120 and 87: Our recommendation is to wait to become pregnant until you have the troubled parts of your career sorted out. Go back over the test to determine what career areas are giving you the most problems. This kind of score indicates the need for marked changes in your career pattern, but if you make a game plan for yourself, with a realistic timetable, you needn't have to wait too long to become pregnant.

If you've decided that you want to have children and now is the right time in your career to do it, think about the quality of the time and the kind of life you'll have as a career mother. We firmly believe in asking ourselves lots of questions before making a major life decision. We've prepared a checklist for you to use to determine where and how your life will change when your baby comes.

Am I Prepared for When the Baby Comes?

1. How good am I at shifting gears? Being a career woman, wife, and mother will mean at least two shifting of gears a day, one when I come home from work and spend time with my child, another when baby is in bed and I become wife to my husband.

2. Even if you have full-time help (which is difficult to find and expensive to maintain), there will still be things you'll want to do for your child, from giving a bath to reading a bedtime story. You'll also want to be available if your child needs you during the day. If you had to, could you leave work in the middle of the day without causing a problem?

3. Will you have the time and desire to participate in some of your child's activities, from Little League to scouting?

4. Deep down inside you, where you live, which comes first: your child or your career? Of course, you can have it all, but having children calls for flexibility, and you may have to trade off a major advancement that involves extensive travel or longer hours for a year or two, until your child or children are older. Would you be willing to do that?

5. Who will be responsible for the details of your child's life, such as doctor's appointments, choosing the right school, chauffeuring him or her around?
    a. Will it be totally your responsibility?
    b. Will you and your husband share it?
    c. Will you use some kind of outside help or cooperative arrangement with other working mothers to form car pools and baby-sitting teams?

6. Do you have the kind of career you can pursue at home or on a part-time or free-lance basis? Writers, artists, photographers, teachers, college professors, lawyers, accountants, and many other professionals can work at home or during hours that work best for their schedules.

7. Would you be comfortable working at home, or do you need an office environment to function?

8. If you or your husband or both of you envision several job relocations in the future, how will that affect your child? People who have children do relocate, of course, but it makes the process more complex when you have a family. In addition to finding two jobs in the same city, you'll have to find the right neighborhood for your children, the right schools and support systems, etc.

9. Do you need a lot of time by yourself? If so, how will you deal with the lack or reduction of it when you have a child?
10. You and your husband will still want time alone together. How will you schedule and manage it?
11. If your career or his involves a lot of business socializing after work, how will you manage those activities and time with your child?
12. Do you often bring work home in the evening? How will you juggle that work and spend time with your family at the end of the day?
13. Do you or your mate have hobbies and interests? Will you still have time to pursue them after the birth of your child? If not, would you be willing to give them up?
14. Finally, have you both agreed that whatever changes will have to be made to ensure a quality life for your child, you'll both make them willingly and happily?

Being a mother is a career in itself, requiring the commitment, the knowledge, the skills, and the understanding that you would bring to any career. If you decide to have children and maintain your career, you will, in effect, have decided on having two careers. Can you handle that kind of dual commitment? Mothering is not just a wonderful experience; it's a full-time responsibility.

Many women are opting today to continue working after the birth of a child. We know one woman who was back at work four days after her child was born. Other women may take anywhere from two weeks to a year, but it is clearly in the maternity leave category, not a decision to leave work and stay home with their children.

We know two women, both dedicated journalists, one with five years' experience and the other with eleven years' experience. They both have had children in the last two years, and both have stopped working. Each wrote a series of articles, for different newspapers, on the joys of motherhood. They were truly beautiful stories, touching on the unique experiences a mother has watching her child grow, from the first time his or her eyes focus on you to the first grip of tiny fingers touching yours. How much of that do you yourself want to experience? If you want to stay at home until your child is of school age, what will that do to your career? What are you willing to trade off, going back to the Pay to Play Principle?

Be flexible enough to change your mind about how you want to rear your child. We know one woman who was determined to stay at home for the first five years. Two months after her child was born, she fell into a postpartum depression. It persisted for several months, no matter how she tried to cope. She finally faced the fact that she didn't want to stay at home; she wanted to go back to work. She found a wonderful older woman who would take care of her daughter, along with two or three other children of preschool ages, during the workday. She was able to drop her daughter off on the way to work and pick her up on the way home. Her depression lifted, and she found she enjoyed her daughter more, because she no longer felt trapped by her. Today Samantha is a lively five-year-old who seems to bear no scars from her mother's decision to go back to work.

Children need a happy environment in which to thrive. If the way in which you thought you wanted to deal with motherhood isn't making you happy, change it. It will make your life—and your child's life—much happier.

Taking Care of Yourself While You're Pregnant

The first thing to remember is that pregnancy is a condition, not a disease. You needn't treat yourself as if you're ill.

Bettye's theory is that you should treat yourself with as little deference as possible when you're pregnant. "The bigger deal you make out of it, the more you'll be singled out for special attention—which is exactly what you don't want," she says.

Since Bettye was divorced during her pregnancy, she had to deal with it on her own, and she found some benefits to it. "I had no one to pay me homage, no one to cry to, and no one to humor through the supposed many moods of pregnancy. Therefore,

I simply did not give in to the waves of self-pity that would some-times wash over me; I simply couldn't."

For some women, there can be physical and emotional com-plications caused by pregnancy. It's possible that you could have to stop working for a period of time should any complication develop. Discuss the possibilities and options with your doctor. Don't an-ticipate trouble, but be prepared for it, and build in the flexibility you may need should you have to take a leave of absence during as well as after your pregnancy.

"Fortunately," says Bettye, "I had a pregnancy with no com-plications, so my health didn't suffer at all. In a normal pregnancy, such as the one I had, there's no reason to over-discuss it, particu-larly in your business situation. Tell your boss and your staff when appropriate, but other than that, my advice would be to let the rest of the world hear it through the grapevine. Be happy; thank people when they congratulate you; then go about your usual business schedule."

Although you'll want to cope well with your pregnancy, you'll need to acknowledge to yourself that it's a time of great change in your life. From cosmetic issues, like gaining weight, to new feelings about the life growing inside you, there's a lot to think about and deal with. Lean on your support systems a little. Certainly, involve your husband as much as possible in the new feelings you're ex-periencing. You'll not only get his support but be able to share your pregnancy and the coming birth of your child with him. Friends can be very helpful and supportive. So can family. The only peo-ple to avoid are the women who seem to delight in telling pregnant women scare stories about their own pregnancies or childbirths. For some reason, there are women out there who seem to enjoy frightening mothers-to-be. Try to avoid them. If you find yourself in conversation with someone who persists in telling you about her twenty-hour pain-filled labor, don't hesitate to cut her off, stating firmly that you're not really interested in those kinds of stories. And walk away. The best person to advise you about what to expect during your pregnancy and childbirth is your doctor. He or she is the one who knows your medical history and has the best, most current information on all the medical facts you'll need to know.

Choosing the right doctor is critical. Try to use a doctor who is referred to you by someone you trust. Ideally, if you have a good general practitioner or internist whose judgment you value, ask him or her for recommendations. If not, ask friends who've had good experiences whom they used. Then check out the doctor yourself. Find out what hospital he or she is affiliated with. Does it have the best facilities for childbirth and any complications that could occur? Is it conveniently located? How are its staff and services rated?

Make an appointment to talk with the doctor who has been recommended before you become his patient. For career women, it is crucial to have a doctor who understands and believes in women working while they are pregnant and after the birth of the baby. If you have a doctor who is antagonistic to one or both of these circumstances, he will create obstacles for you instead of helping you cope and find solutions.

Other factors need to be considered. For example, if you want to have your child by the Lamaze method or some form of natural childbirth, is your doctor in agreement with it? Does he believe in the father of the child's being involved in the pregnancy and birth?

Most important of all, is he or she a straight shooter, who will tell you all you need to know and who will answer all your questions with facts, not with "It's nothing to worry your little head over."

Once you've found the right doctor, a major problem has been solved. You have now done everything you can to ensure good prenatal and postnatal care of your baby.

Consult with your doctor on whether any changes in your schedule or your lifestyle need to be made to accommodate your pregnancy. Remember that each pregnancy is different, so don't judge what you ought to do by what friends have done. We know a woman, pregnant with her first child at the age of thirty-eight, who for the first three months of her pregnancy was tired all the time and slept most of the day. She had always been an energetic, high-powered woman, her life filled with activities. Suddenly she was bedridden for most of three months. Fortunately she had a good doctor, who explained to her that some pregnancies are like this and that for the first three months she would just have to accept it. Sure enough, at the beginning of her fourth month, her energy returned.

Ask your doctor about diet and nutrition. Describe your present eating habits to him, and ask him whether you're eating right. Ask him to prescribe the proper diet or supplemental vitamins if he thinks they're called for.

Make sure you're getting enough sleep and enough rest. If you lead a busy, active life, you may be used to squeaking by on the minimum amount of sleep, but you may find you need more during your pregnancy. If you do, make sure you get it. Rest is very important. Aside from preserving your physical strength, resting quietly provides a good opportunity to sort out your thoughts and feelings, keep in touch with yourself, throw off the burdens of the workday, and just commune with yourself.

As your body changes and expands during pregnancy, you will need some maternity clothes. Thankfully, today women have a wide choice of clothing, much of which is skillfully designed to minimize their pregnant figures and to keep them looking trim for most of the months of their pregnancies. Plug into your friends on this one to find out what their best sources were for clothes that are fashionable but comfortable, wear well, and make you feel you look your best while your body is changing.

Bettye employed another strategy that may work for you. She simply wore clothes that were two or three sizes larger than the ones she normally wore. "During the last three months of my pregnancy, I simply wore size tens," she says. "I was lucky enough to have some contributions from my mother and some friends, and I bought some casual clothes at a maternity shop, but by and large, I made it through on my size tens. Believe me, afterward you never want to see any of those clothes again because you've worn them so much, so don't get all hung up on buying things you can use when the pregnancy is over."

Keep up your beauty and grooming regimen, and do exercises regularly, subject, of course, to your doctor's approval. Indulge yourself a little as you get into the last couple of months of pregnancy, when your added weight and ballooning figure may drag you down. Get a new hairstyle. Have a facial. Do whatever you need to do to feel good about your physical self.

If you work with a lot of men, be prepared for some of them to feel protective of you as your pregnancy advances. Some may even treat you like a china doll that may break. Their concern is well motivated, if misplaced in a business situation. Treat them kindly, but let them know you're not all that fragile, you're not ill, you're pregnant, and you're perfectly all right. If you pursue business as usual, they'll follow suit.

Use the pregnancy period to plan, plan, plan. Read everything you can possibly get your hands on about children and babies. Consult your doctor, your local librarian, and friends to compile a reading list. Remember, everyone has his or her own theory, so make your own judgments on what you read, and synthesize what you've learned into a theory of your own with which you feel comfortable. Keep all the books as reference material because things will change constantly. Just at the time you think you've got little Johnny all figured out, he will change drastically. Of course, being a mother for the first time is a learning experience, so be prepared to revise some of your theories as you go.

Your planning doesn't end with a book list. If you need a bigger home or apartment to accommodate the new baby, look for one during the early months of your pregnancy. Try to be fully settled in by the time you give birth. Enough change will be happening to you without the additional change of a new home. If you need to add a room or convert one into a nursery, do this in time to leave the last couple of months hassle-free.

If you know you will need part-time or full-time help with ır child, begin investigating your options. Get leads on the very best personnel agencies in town that deal with help. Place an ad of your own in the local newspaper looking for help, and check references very, very carefully. Meet with your job candidate several times before making a final decision. Once you know that the person is reliable, you will probably want to check into background, values, and attitudes. After all, you are hiring someone who will be a major influence on your child's life. You want to be sure that the values and attitudes he or she communicates are ones that you agree with and want taught to your child.

Plan how your days will be organized if you are going back to work shortly after the birth of your baby. Will you have some time in the morning to spend with your child? Time in the evening? How will you and your husband manage time alone together? If you are a person who absolutely needs some time alone each day, how will you manage it?

Make sure all the decisions you make about how your life will change—who your help will be and what your schedule will be like—are fully discussed with your husband. To work, these decisions must be joint ones. After all, if you are going to be rearranging his life as well as yours, he should have an equal say in how it's done.

Another thing to plan on is total flexibility. All your ability to turn on a dime that you've brought to play in your job will be needed to an even greater degree when you have a child. A child won't always follow your schedule or do what you want to do when you want to do it.

We've prepared a set of guidelines for organizing your time so that you'll have the time you need for career, husband, and children. Remember, you'll have to make some trade-offs and remain flexible. But before you can change how you use your time, you need to analyze the time you have and how you use it now. Then determine what you want to change, adding or deleting things as you go. We've based our guidelines on the total number of hours there are in a month. Once you've worked out a monthly schedule, convert it to a day-by-day schedule. Use it as a guide, not a straightjacket. And dust off your sense of humor; you'll need it. Children tend to do unpredictable things at the most inconvenient times. You'll just have to cope with a smile.

Some Guidelines for Managing Your Time

The management of time operates exactly like the management of money. People with loads of time, like people with loads of money, don't really need to account for where it all goes. However, as a career mother, you can bet that there is a distinct shortage of time in your life, and therefore, you need to budget your time carefully, or you just won't be able to accomplish what you need to.

The formula for budgeting your time is easy. Take it in steps.

Step I: Categorize the activities that are part of your life by listing them on a piece of paper—be specific.

Step II: After making the first list, write the same list on another sheet of paper, adding the exact average number of hours per month you spend on each activity. Include an explanation where necessary. This explanation step is important because it will help you when you start analyzing how you spend your time.

Step III: There are, on the average, 730 hours per month. Take the total number of hours per month you need for your activities, and subtract it from 730.

Step IV: Now analyze the results. Don't be discouraged if there are fewer hours in the month than you need to do all the things you want to do. Go back over your list. We'll discuss some hints on how to analyze what you see.

Let's use one career mother as an example and follow her through this time management exercise. Cynthia is married, has two small children, and lives in a large metropolitan area. Her husband is an investment banker, and they both travel a moderate amount in their business.

STEP I
Categorize the activities in your life; no particular order is necessary. Cynthia came up with the following list:

1. Work
2. Time with children
3. Time with husband
4. Running the household. In being very specific, Cynthia broke this category down as follows:
   —instructions to the housekeeper
   —shopping for household provisions
   —entertaining
   —laundry
   —weekend duties (cleaning, etc.)
   —clothes shopping
5. Business travel
6. Paying bills/balancing family checkbook
7. Commutation to and from work
8. Getting the children off to school
9. Personal hygiene (includes getting ready for work in the morning, any regular exercise, and nighttime beauty routine)
10. Hairdresser
11. Nonbusiness luncheons
12. Nonbusiness dinners
13. Reading business-related material
14. Reading nonbusiness-related material
15. Sleep
16. Meal preparation and eating
17. Relaxing
18. Medical care
19. Miscellaneous, broken down as follows:
    —telephone time
    —play with the dog
    —children's school activities

Where the Time Goes	Step II (Cynthia's analysis) Commentary	Avg. No. of Hours Per Month
1. Work	Averaging a ten-hour day	217
2. Time with children	Spent playing with the children after work, reading stories, talking about school, etc.	115
3. Time with husband	Solo time spent with spouse in the care and feeding of the marriage	44
4. Running the household		
—housekeeper instructions		3
—shopping for household provisions		4
—entertaining	Having people over for drinks and dinner . . . figuring an average of twice a week	17
—laundry	Arranging, sorting, and having pickups and deliveries	1
—weekend duties (cleaning, etc.)	Time spent keeping the household together when the housekeeper is not working	30
—clothes and present shopping		1
5. Business travel	In addition to work, sleep, etc., while on a business trip. This is flying, traveling time . . .	6
6. Paying bills/family finances	Keeping the budget straight, balancing the checkbook	2

Where the Time Goes	Commentary	Avg. No. of Hours Per Month
7. Commutation to and from work	This is the actual time it takes to go door to door, home to office, and return. (This time can be used effectively in some other activity. Cynthia uses it to talk with her husband, since they commute together; many read, work, etc.)	22
8. Getting the children ready for school	Prior to arrival of housekeeper . . . prepare lunches, getting dressed, etc.	10
9. Personal hygiene	Getting ready for work in the morning, occasional long baths, once-a-month facial and manicure	24
10. Hairdresser	One visit per month	2
11. Luncheons (nonbusiness)	Saturday luncheons with friends	4
12. Dinners (nonbusiness)	Weekly dinners with friends, outside the home; otherwise, it goes into entertainment catgory	52
13. Reading (business)	Time spent at home on business-oriented periodicals and books	8
14. Reading (nonbusiness)	Basically what you do to relax. In this particular case, Cynthia does a lot of reading, which is her form of relaxation	20
15. Sleep	Averaging seven hours per night	212

Where the Time Goes	Commentary	Avg. No. of Hours Per Month
16. Meal preparation and eating	Those nights when they don't go out or entertain	35
17. Relaxing	Doing nothing	12
18. Medical care	Taking children or self to doctor, dentist	1
19. Miscellaneous	Try to define everything	2
—telephone time to parents		
—playing with the dog		
—children's school activities		

STEP III
Total your hours, and subtract from the average number of hours in a month, 730. In Cynthia's case, her total was 844. Obviously, a problem. Hence, the most important next step: ANALYZE!

STEP IV
Analyze your results.
1. Go back over your list, and ask yourself the following questions:
   —Have I added anything that I really don't do or don't spend as much time on as I initially thought?
   —Do I have any duplication? The commuting example is typical. Often you can do something else while you are commuting to work; have you counted those hours twice? Are you separating (as Cynthia was doing) meal preparation, quality time with her children, and communication with her husband when in reality you are doing all three at once . . . none probably very well?
2. Now go down the list and make a sublist of all the items where you spend the greatest amount of your time. For Cynthia it would be:
   —Work   217
   —Sleep   212
   —Child care   115
   —Dinners (nonbusiness)   52
   —Husband care   44
   —Meal preparation   35
   —Cleaning (weekends)   30
   Analyze the big numbers for areas you can cut, keeping in mind to cut where you want to cut first . . . meaning to cut the things that don't particularly give you pleasure. Look at the numbers for realism. Can Cynthia really be spending 115 hours per month on quality time with her children? She should take this number and break it down more, to determine if she is kidding herself or not.

3. Take the list again, and make another sublist of all the items on which you spend small amounts of time, but which add up over the course of the month.

List time, again in descending order of amount of time:

—Personal hygiene	24
—Reading (nonbusiness)	20
—Home entertaining	17
—Getting children ready for school	10
—Reading (business)	8
—Business travel	6
—Shopping for household	4
—Luncheons (nonbusiness)	4
—Housekeeper instructions	3
—Paying bills	2
—Miscellaneous	2
—Hairdresser	2
—Laundry	1
—Clothes/present shopping	1
—Medical care	1
—Relaxing	½

This exercise may in itself seem like a lot of duplication, but it is *the* way for you to get an exact handle on your time management problems. Now look closely at this list. On this list there should be small items you can delegate to one of several people: (1) a housekeeper; (2) older children; or (3) your husband. For example, in Cynthia's case, there is no reason that the paying of bills, shopping for household goods, and some part of other chores, such as getting the children ready for school, the laundry, etc., could not be chores shared with her husband.

In many cases, until this kind of close analysis takes place, one spouse does not realize how much of the burden is being borne by the other spouse. This clearly defines the situation in black and white.

You must work and juggle with the numbers until you get within the budget of 730. At that point you should feel in control. If you get that "out of control feeling" again, go back and re-analyze and reperform the exercise.

Next, make a day-to-day schedule, referring back to your monthly breakdown of hours, to make sure you're accomplishing daily what you need to.

Options for Child Care

If you have made the decision to maintain a career while rearing a child (or two or more children), then you have also decided to have some kind of help with caring for your child, whether you choose a day care center, part-time or full-time help, a person in the community who will watch two or three children at once during the day at her home, or a nursery or preschool. More informally, you may have a mother or other relative who is willing to play the role of surrogate mother while you and your husband are at work. Another option recently available to women is that they split child care duties with their mates, either by both of them taking part-time jobs or working different shifts or by doing the kind of work that can be scheduled around child care, e.g., writing, teaching at a college. If you and your husband are in that situation, you can have the best of all possible worlds: two-parent parenting.

Traditionally child care has largely been the mother's responsibility, with the father playing a supporting, but lesser, role. Today more and more fathers want to participate in bringing up their children, and if their work hours permit daytime contact, all the better for the two-career couple with children—and all the better for the children, according to several recent studies which found that children benefit from close contact with both parents.

However, even though some couples can now work joint parenting around their careers, most still aren't in the position to solve the problem of child care by splitting the tasks between them. If you and your husband have traditional nine-to-five jobs, you will have to find someone other than yourselves to help.

In the section on taking care of yourself, we mentioned using personnel agencies in looking for full- or part-time nursing or governess help. You can also ask your doctor if there is anyone he or she can recommend. Plug into friends—they may know of some person or service that can help. Some cities and towns have a kind of day care hot line you can call for day care facilities in your area. But plan way ahead on this since there is usually a waiting list, especially in large urban centers. Check carefully the cost and quality of the child care. Does the facility allow any flexibility in scheduling? Some day care centers are very strict about children being picked up on time—can you guarantee that every day at four or five you will be there?

It's very important to find the kind of child care help that suits your careers and, more important, what you want for your child. If you are affiliated with a religious group or church, sometimes it has child care facilities, or your minister may be able to recommend several organizations you can go to for help.

You and your husband need to be totally comfortable with whatever your final choice is for day care. If you are choosing a person to be a part-time or full-time live-in surrogate mother, you must be totally at home and at ease with her, especially if she will be sharing your home.

Bettye has full-time live-in help, and she and Charlie are totally comfortable with it.

On the other hand, another woman we know—we'll call her Carol—had a different experience. For the years when her three children were very young, Carol had full-time help that went home at the end of each day. The children loved their nurse so much they called her Nanny, and now that the children are grown, they still keep in touch with her. When Nanny left, Carol tried a succession of live-in nurses—four of them. None was quite right.

One was too lenient and let the children run wild all day. Another was used to having servants herself and spent most of her time with Carol being taken care of because she had a bad back. Another just wasn't good with the children. And so on. Finally, her oldest daughter, twelve at the time, said, "Mom, I think I can handle things from the time I get home from school until you get home from work [approximately three hours each day]." Of course, all three children were in school by then—the youngest was eight—and she had helpful neighbors who kept an eye out and were available just in case there was a problem, but the system worked much better than having live-in help.

"I enjoyed my children and my whole life at home so much more after we got rid of our live-in help," Carol says. "I was never comfortable having someone who wasn't part of my family sharing my home. My husband and children were happier, too."

You just have to decide what's right for you. If you think you want full-time live-in help, investigate the cost and the availability, and then really analyze whether you'd like someone sharing your home.

If full-time help is not for you, perhaps part-time help is the answer, either someone who can stay with your child during work hours or someone who will take care of your child at her home during work hours.

If neither of those is right, check out day care facilities. They vary widely in quality, so judge each one on its own.

Arrange interviews with the people who run the facility, meet the person or people who will actually take care of your child, and ask to observe for a few hours or for a day, to get a feel for the atmosphere. You owe it to yourself and to your child to know exactly what kind of environment you're choosing for him or her. And it will give you tremendous peace of mind if you truly trust the people who are going to be surrogate parents to your child.

As your child grows, he or she will develop ideas, feelings, and preferences of his or her own. If your child decides he is not happy in whatever child care situation you've chosen, listen to what he has to say. What he's objecting to may be something that's easily resolved or just needs being explained to him in order for him to feel comfortable. On the other hand, he may have some legitimate reasons to ask you to change the arrangements. Even though you like the person or facility you've chosen, if your child is unhappy, it's not the right solution.

The other extreme is when your child develops a deep and strong attachment to his surrogate parent, especially if you have full-time help. Be prepared for the time your child asks for the nurse before he asks for you. Try not to be hurt, but to understand, since you're the one who has opted for a surrogate parent.

When your child reaches school age, you will need to choose schools as carefully as you have chosen child care. You may opt for the local public school, after investigating its facilities and the quality of the education, or you may opt for a private school. Either way you will have to research carefully. And you will probably still need some part-time help to bridge the hours between the end of the schoolday and the end of your workday.

If you work all day, what do you do on the nights when you want to go out without the children?

For starters, don't feel guilty, unless you get the urge to go out every night. Even if you have children, you and your husband need and deserve your time alone together; you need time with friends, time to share new experiences unrelated to home or to work. Unless you have live-in help, you will need to have a list of reliable baby-sitters. Neighborhood teenagers can be good, or a retired senior citizen, your mother or grandmother, or someone else's. Having a list is important because it gives you flexibility. You shouldn't depend on one baby-sitter's always being free when you need her, especially if she's good. Sometimes you can build a baby-sitting network of neighborhood mothers who may be interested in cooperative baby-sitting. Each of you may be willing to offer one night a week for the good of the group.

Finding the right child care is crucially important. We've prepared a checklist on how to find the right people or services to care for your child.

Choosing the Right Child Care

This is the one subject of major concern to every working mother. Be realistic about what your choices are on the basis of your economic situation. The main options are:

Housekeeper/nurse—live-in
Housekeeper/nurse—live-out
Baby-sitter (you take the child to another location daily)
Baby-sitter (comes to your house after school daily)
A relative who lives close by
Day care or preschool facility

To make the right choice from the options open to you, carefully analyze the following:

1. Realistically, what can you afford? Write down a specific amount which your budget will allow you to pay for child care.
2. Investigate your market. Find out what you will get for the amount you can afford. Use the following resources:
   a. Talk to friends who have help; ask friends to talk to other friends; put your dilemma out on the grapevine.
   b. Call a few domestic agencies, and test the amount you can afford with them.
   c. If you don't have any other way of investigating, run an ad in the local newspaper spelling out exactly what you want and what you can pay. See what kind of response you get. You'll know quickly.
3. Now that you know your options, look inside yourself and ask, "what arrangement will give me the most comfort, the most security?" Break it down further by answering these subquestions:

—What arrangement best suits the way we live?

—How does my husband feel?

—What arrangement works best for what I want to do for my child?

—What trade-offs am I willing to make?

4. When you know your options and your needs (and if you've decided to use someone other than a relative to care for your child), it's time to start interviewing candidates. Be tough in your interviews. After all, the person you hire will take care of that child who is so precious to you. We've put together some guidelines for interviewing child care personnel.

Interview Guidelines

It's best to have candidates come to your home at a time when your child is awake, so they can meet each other and so that you observe their reactions to each other.

—Does the candidate seem warm and loving?

—Does she seem shy and hesitant to touch your child?

—Does your child ignore her, reach for her, run from her? Watch all the reactions closely. They may not mean much, but they are certainly valuable indicators.

—Make the candidate feel as comfortable as possible, so that you can observe her at her best.

I. HISTORY QUESTIONS

You need to know the background of every candidate you interview, especially previous work experience. Where has she worked before? For whom? How long? What were her duties? Why is she leaving the position? Can you check with her employer? Go back at least five years to get a picture of what she's actually been doing with her life. If she says this is her first venture into the field of child care, ask her what other kind of work she's done, and ask for references. Were there children involved in this other kind of work? If so, what kind of rapport did she have with them? Why did she leave?

Take notes during the interview, so you can refer back to them later, check references, etc.

II. THEORY QUESTIONS

After you ask questions about the candidate's history and job experience, you'll want to know her views on how children ought to be cared for, to make sure her theory of child care matches (or is close to) yours. Ask her:

—What do you feel is the most important thing to give a baby?
—Should a baby be allowed to cry at all?
—What about sleep habits? If a baby cries during the night, what do you think should happen?
—How do you feel about discipline? What form should it take?
—If you were bringing up a child of your own, what would you do first, second, etc.? (The point of this question is to learn her priorities.)
—How do you feel about reading to a child?
—What do you feel you do best with children?

III. EXPLAIN YOUR SITUATION

Be clear about exactly what you are looking for, what the requirements and the hours of the job will be. If your theories and hers don't match, probe for substantive differences. If they're there, go on to your next candidate. You don't want someone feeding your child values and attitudes that contradict your own. Be very specific about all the details. If she will live in and you think she's a possibility, show her the living arrangements. If she will live out, explain the hours clearly. Talk about how she is going to get back and forth from work. The more information you can gather in your interview, the less likely you are to make a mistake in your final choice. Talk about the cleaning, the laundry, and any other chores she will be expected to do. If there are household pets, be sure she is introduced, and see how they react to one another. If she is to have any responsibility for them, explain thoroughly. Explain the pay system, Social Security, and any other deductions clearly. Be very definite about how much she will take home each payday; establish the payday.

IV. CHECK REFERENCES

If you like the candidate and want to consider her, tell her exactly when you will let her know if she has the job. Get specific references, complete with names, addresses, and telephone numbers. Do the reference check thoroughly, using the following procedure as a guideline.

When you reach the person given as a reference, explain your situation thoroughly: "I'm Mary Jones of Smith Street in New York. Muriel Watson has applied for a job as housekeeper to take care of my four-year-old son. She will live out and come five days a week. Since I work, I'll be leaving my son in her care all day. I want to know as much as I can about her. Would you tell me please when and for how long she worked for you?

—"What exactly were her responsibilities?"
—"How was she with the children?"
—"Was she ever out sick? How often?"
—"Does she have any personal problems that would interfere with her getting her work done?"
—"Why did she leave you? Would you rehire her?"
—"Are there any problem areas I should be aware of?"
—"What did other members of the family think of her?"

Take notes during the reference check. Go back over what you found out. Check the next reference, using the same questions. If you found a weakness in the candidate in talking to the first reference, mention it to the second reference, and ask whether she can confirm it. For example, "I noticed that Muriel seems a bit rigid in her theories of child rearing. Did you ever have any problems with that rigidity?"

If the references are satisfactory, you have found a housekeeper. If not, keep looking. You need to judge the person by her history, and if everything doesn't meet your standards, it's better to pass.

This is difficult to do when you're desperate. Our advice: Take every precaution you can to prevent yourself from being in a desperate situation, in which you may have to settle for someone who really isn't what you want for your child.

While you are looking for the primary caretaker, keep your eyes open for people who may be good on a part-time or baby-sitting basis, and ask them if they're ever available for that kind of work. Keep telephone numbers and names. Ask them about relatives who might be interested in some part-time work. Keep those numbers, too. The more child care resources you have, the more options you have, and the less likely you are to find yourself in a desperate situation.

Check with schools in your neighborhood. Older children are often available for after-school assistance and summer help. Depending on the age of your child, this system can work well as a backup in a crisis.

Form a network of other career mothers who live in your neighborhood. Help each other out in times of crisis by watching each others' children. The more you know, and the more names and numbers you keep, the easier it will be to find a backup system in a crisis.

V. REVIEWING YOUR OPTIONS

As time goes on, your options and requirements for child care will change. Be flexible. If you discover a better way, pursue it. If your financial situation improves, upgrade your child care if you think it could be better. The point is to review periodically whatever system you have to make sure you're still on the right track.

Getting Away with the Children

Taking time out to spend exclusively with your children is important. Whether it's a day, a weekend, or an annual family vacation, getting away is a good solution to leaving everyday cares behind and enjoying new experiences together. Depending on the age of your child or children, places like amusement parks, zoos, historical sites, museums, natural wonders—you name it—are fun to visit together. A "doing things" vacation—like a camping or fishing trip—can be fun if those are things you and your husband enjoy. If they aren't and you do them just for the kids, they'll sense you're faking it, and you've just defeated the purpose of getting away together. Besides, there are enough things the whole family can enjoy that there's no need for anyone to "suffer through" a family getaway.

In addition to taking time out or a vacation with the children, you may find it important to have equal time away from the children with your husband, putting the emphasis on the relationship between the two of you. Many career couples we know who have children take two vacations a year, one with the kids and one without. Of course, as children get older, there are places they can go without you, such as summer camp, a tour of the country or of Europe, or class or organization trips that may take them away for a day or a week. In that way, everyone in the family gets a separate vacation.

Judge what's right for you. If you love to be surrounded by your family all the time, you may not need two vacations or three; one may be just fine. If you need time away from your children, be sure you get it because you need it and because it will improve the quality of the time you do spend with your children.

A long-term benefit of doing things together as a family is that you will be exposing your children to new sights, new experiences, new hobbies, and new interests.

Carol and her husband took their children to Europe every year for several years. They would concentrate on one or two countries each trip. Carol would fully research each country and make notes on what they would see. She acted as tour guide for the whole family and made the trips an educational as well as a fun experience. Today all three of her grown children are experienced European travelers. They all are also wonderful skiers because for years Carol and her husband have owned a ski house in Vermont. The ski house came about because Carol's husband, Roy, loved to ski. Carol was determined that she and the children should be with him, so they all learned to ski and eventually bought the house.

"The beauty of it is," Carol, a vice-president of a major firm, "we all get what we want. I'm not that avid a skier, but because we have the house, I can ski or I can read, cook, walk in the woods, or visit with the many friends we've made in our ski community. The kids have been able to use the house on school vacations, and Roy gets to do as much skiing as he wants."

If you're working on a tight budget, a possible solution is to combine business travel with a family vacation. If you or your husband are traveling in some other state or country on business, have the family join you. The cost is less because it is only the extra airfare and any extra nights of accommodation not covered by the business trip.

If you don't do any business travel, there are still many things to do and see that are relatively inexpensive and closer to home. The point is to get away from it all as a family.

Getting into Gear as a Family

At work all day you deal with adults, and although some of those adults can act in pretty strange ways, usually there is a predictability to their behavior. Basically you control your workday and your work environment. In fact, as a career woman you pride yourself on your ability to control.

Forget all that when you go home to your child or children at night. As any child psychologist will tell you, children go through stages. Just as you think you've got your child all figured out, he's off and running into another stage. Be flexible, mom; there's more to come. Right through adolescence, children's attitudes, values, and behavior patterns change. And you'll have to allow for that change, encouraging the good things, discouraging anything that seems bad, and making the best of all of it. That's the bad news. The good news is that each stage brings a new kind of enjoyment, a new sense of discovering another aspect of this person who is your child. If you keep your eyes open and maintain a sense of humor and perspective, you can learn a lot. But don't expect predictability. Kids are sure to surprise you.

Leave your desire to control everything and everyone at the office. At home you'll need to become master of the fine arts of listening, understanding, and compromise. If you try to fit your child into slots of accepted behavior, you may be happy in the short term, but your child will feel stifled. There needs to be a lot of give-and-take in a parent/child relationship, and parents need to give children growing room or they'll feel cramped. Basically children respond to love, discipline, caring, and nurturing. They do not respond to sustained control.

Home is the place for relaxation and enjoyment. To ensure that it is, apply the Shifting Gears Principle, and multiply its effectiveness geometrically when you have children.

Children expect—and deserve—your attention when you get home at the end of the day. In order to make that time count, you need to prepare yourself mentally to move from the world of business to the world of children. Whether it's playing hide-and-go-seek with your three-year-old or discussing the new math with your eight-year-old, you need to be *there*, mentally as well as physically. If you're bored or distracted or tense, children will know it instantly. Although you may be saying you want to be with them, you're also sending the contradictory message of "Leave me alone."

It's not easy to leave work behind you at the end of the day, but in order to manage successfully being a parent as well as a career woman, you need to find a system that lets you do it, whether it's walking home from work to have time to shift gears, sitting quietly in your office for a few minutes at the end of the day, catching your breath and getting ready to go home—whatever "trick" works for you. When you walk through that door, your attention should be focused on your children.

Bettye and Charlie spend their first hour and a half at home every night with Ashley. She knows it's her time, and she gets to choose how they spend it, whether it's playing a game or just talking about the day.

"We take no phone calls, we read no mail, we don't even talk to each other, except through Ashley, during that period every night," Bettye says.

Another couple we know uses the family dinnertime for a round-table discussion, with family members talking about their day, exchanging ideas on topics from politics to sports. They strive to keep dinnertime a special family time, with no interruptions.

Find the system that works for you to ensure that you spend quality time, on a daily basis, with your children.

The Single Parent

In the last few years there have been a number of women—and some men—who have decided to become single parents. It can be done, but it's very difficult and you need to plan out carefully how you will care for a child, financially and physically, while maintaining a career.

Doris, like Bettye, chose to have a child even though her marriage was ending in divorce.

"It was actually my wanting a child that caused the marriage to end. At least it was one of about eighty-four thousand reasons," Doris says. "My ex-husband decided that one of the main reasons we couldn't have a child was that in his opinion I would be an incompetent mother since I wanted to maintain my career. The marriage was ended, but I had my baby anyway. And I haven't regretted it. Sure, it's been hard, but luckily I can afford help, and I've managed. And the positives are all I hoped they would be."

With the high divorce rate, many women are left with children to rear as single parents. Of course, it's not easy, but it can be done. One comfort is that many women have been through it before you and survived and that many women are going through it at the same time you are and somehow they're managing. There are a lot of books on the subject of single parenting which provide some answers to how to deal with being a single parent.

Having been a single parent for a while herself, Bettye can see some advantages in single parenting: "It can be a very strengthening experience to know that you have sole responsibility for your child. And that you can handle it. And you also know, whatever the outcome, it's been primarily your influence that has affected your child. You really can't blame the results of the child rearing on anyone else, and you don't have to share the decision making. Even in the best of marriages, parents can disagree on what is best for their children. When there are two parents, some compromise must be reached. If you're a single parent, you make the final decisions.

"With hindsight, I think my decision to have Ashley alone was right. I didn't want to have her born into the middle of an unhappy marriage on the brink of divorce. However, I don't think I would have liked being alone with her forever. The sharing of the experience of a child with someone you love and who loves your child tremendously is something no mother should miss. On the other hand, if the right person had not appeared, I think I could have done it alone.

"From a support system standpoint, not much has changed with my remarriage. I still need full-time live-in help, and I still bear many of the responsibilities of rearing Ashley, but there is a wonderful sense of sharing it all with my husband that makes it that much more rewarding."

Most mothers become single parents after a divorce or the death of a husband. In addition to having to assume the full responsibility for their children, they have to explain why the marriages ended or deal with the children's pain at the deaths of their fathers. A key here is to listen to your children, to figure out what they want to know and need to know right then. Depending on their ages, you may want to tell them everything or very little. If you're confused as to what to tell them, how to deal with their pain and grief, discuss it with some friends, or seek professional help from a counselor or minister. Remember, dealing through strength means being able to ask for help without feeling you're weak.

Just as you are going through the trauma of change in your life, so are your children. You need to show them as much consistency, continuity, and stability as possible to help them get through this period of change while keeping intact their sense of security. Take your cues from them. Children's needs will vary.

When you're a single parent, you need to organize your time extremely well because there is no other parent with whom to share the responsibilities. Your support systems can help, especially friends who care for your children and will do things with them and spend some time with them. Other family members—your parents, brothers, sisters—can help by giving your children a sense of extended family. You may need to spend more time than you usually do with your children during the transition period, just to reassure them that you are not going to leave them, that their home is secure.

That brings us to another tricky issue. There will come a time when you will want to date, to meet men who will become friends, companions, lovers, or even a new husband. It is important for your life to be complete in this way. You can't shut off your social life just because you are a mother. But you need to make your dating as comfortable and as painless for your children as you can. They may feel threatened when you first begin dating, fearing that some- one else—a stranger—will take their place in your heart. You need to reassure them that is not so. On the other hand, you can't allow yourself to give in to emotional blackmail from your children or to any attempts they may make to manipulate you through guilt. You need contact with adults of the opposite sex. You will be happier if you have it, and therefore, they are likely to be happier. If you allow them to keep you from seeking companionship, not only will you be unhappy, but you'll resent them for depriving you of the opportunity to look for personal happiness, for a man you can love and can share with.

You need to give some thought to the ground rules of your dating. It is no longer unusual for people to sleep together before they are married, and you may want to sleep with the new man in your life at some point. How you handle this is important. If the man is someone you have known and dated for a long time, someone who has gotten to know and care for your children, and someone whom your children care for and if he is someone with whom you can envision a future, then having him stay in your home shouldn't be too threatening or confusing. But this is a tricky area. You don't want this man to become a fixture on weekends for several months and then disappear—one man has already disappeared on your children. The best course is to move slowly and cautiously because any decision you make will affect the lives of your children.

The time may come when you want to remarry. No matter how much you love your new man and how much he loves you, it's important that he care deeply for your children and that they care deeply for him in order for him to work out as their new step-father. In the end, you won't be happy if your children aren't happy, so it's best to "audition" the man you want to marry for your children's approval and affection.

When Rebecca and Sam were thinking of marrying, it was very important to her that Sam love her daughter. And it was important that her daughter, Susan, love him. Although Susan resisted the idea at first, simply because it meant change in her life, she finally accepted it because she saw it was what her mother wanted and because Sam was someone she could love, someone she sensed genuinely loved her and was interested in her.

Cathy's second marriage ended in divorce because her husband did not have the same commitment to her children that she did. When one of her sons was in trouble and causing problems, her husband decided to rent a place of his own because family problems were interfering with his work. After Cathy got over the initial hurt and shock, she decided she wouldn't take him back on any terms. If he wasn't committed to her children, then he wasn't committed to her because part of what she was—an important part—was mother to her two sons.

When You're a Stepmother

Second marriages seem to be more common than first marriages these days. And with many second marriages, one or both partners have children from a previous marriage. We've already discussed what happens when a woman has children and remarries. But what happens to a woman with no children of her own who marries a man with children from a former marriage?

Judy is stepmother to two children. Although their mother has custody, Judy and George have the children every other weekend. Judy loves them, takes care of them, but doesn't try to be their mother—they already have one. They accept and love her as their father's wife and as a person they enjoy and have fun with. They probably also love her because she hasn't usurped their mother's role.

Sandra married a man who has three children from his first marriage, one of them a teenaged daughter who lives with them in their two-bedroom apartment.

"We've had our rough times," Sandra says. "For a couple of years we had the kids only on visits, but when Pat came to live with us, that was a whole other adjustment. Bob and I had been used to our privacy, to having our time alone, and suddenly there was another person in our lives. Pat is really a great kid, but she's going through adolescence, and that's rough, not only on her but on us. It's as if, with no experience, suddenly I'm the mother of a teenager. It was hard to know how to cope. At first, we were very permissive. Pat could come and go as she pleased. But that didn't work. She was staying out till all hours, and finally, it came to a head when there was a party at our apartment while we were away. All the anger that I had been trying to hold in came out. And that was probably for the best because it led to a three-way discussion of what would work best for all of us living together.

"Now we have certain house rules. Pat must be home at a certain time. There are no parties when we're not there. We spend time with her, but we also spend time alone. Luckily she is old enough to have friends and interests of her own, so she isn't alone when we're not with her. And luckily Bob and I have a strong enough relationship that we were able to work out the problems before they hurt our marriage."

When you decide to marry a man with children, you need to accept him and his children as a package deal. Whether they live with you or with their mother, they will affect your life and you will affect theirs, so make the choice knowing the consequences and knowing that being a stepmother, although it's not problem-free (and what is?), has its joys and rewards.

Obviously we could fill a book devoted to coping with motherhood as a career woman. What we've done in this chapter is to give some guidelines, outlining the major decisions you'll need to make about having children and some advice on how to make them. The decision to become a parent is a very personal one, so you'll have to apply our general principles to your particular life.

There's probably no better way to end this chapter than with a quote from a young career mother:

"You couldn't have convinced me, on the days when I thought I could never adjust to being a mother as well as being a career woman, that I would reach the point where I'd be proselytizing for having children," Laura says. "It took me two years to get things together enough to really enjoy my daughter. But I'll tell you something. She is my proudest achievement, the greatest joy in my life, someone who has brought my husband and me closer together in a deeper way. Now when women ask me how I manage it, isn't it hard, I just tell them, 'It's really worth it.' "

SIX

WHEN YOU WORK FOR YOURSELF

I've been doing executive recruiting as a partner in my own business for three years. I've worked just as hard as I ever worked for other people; only the satisfaction is much greater. I know that if I put in extra hours, that's money in my pocket. Of course, it hasn't all been terrific. My partner and I really have had some problems, and I plan to start another firm, with another partner, within the next six months. It's really a risk because I'm pregnant with my first child, but I feel now is the right time to get a new firm started with someone I really can work with.

As a writer I'm lucky because I can work at home, make my own hours, and set my own schedule. It also means I can be the kind of mother that I want to be to my nine-year-old daughter. I'm there when she leaves for school in the morning, and I'm there when she gets home in the afternoon. My peak work periods are between nine in the morning and three in the afternoon. When my daughter comes home, I'm ready for company. We spend time together; then I get dinner going so that when my husband gets home, we have the evening together.

I'm at a real turning point in my life now. I have to decide whether I really want to continue working my way up the corporate ladder or whether I want to work for myself. I know you never get rich working for other people. Besides, I've never been very good at corporate gamesmanship. The idea of striking out on my own is very appealing. But I know it can be scary, too, to leave behind the security of someone else's business to start risking my own money on my ability. And I know I'll miss the camaraderie which I've always enjoyed as part of working in a large office. But I also know that if I don't make the break now, I probably never will. The salary and fringe benefits just get so appealing that you can't afford to walk away.

WORKING FOR YOURSELF—whether you're a one-person industry working at home or you've started your own business—can be a challenging, exciting way to have it all. For those women with the entrepreneurial instinct, it's hard to resist. And there are quite a few well-known role models for women who want to strike out on their own, among them Mary Wells Lawrence, who has built an advertising empire, and Mary Kay of Mary Kay Cosmetics, who made selling makeup at house parties a big business. In the creative arts, writers, from the Brontë sisters to Agatha Christie to Erica Jong, have earned fame and fortune by writing at home.

As with every other aspect of having it all, the Pay to Play Principle applies. There are trade-offs that the entrepreneurial woman must be willing to make if she wants to work for herself. In this chapter we'll talk about the pluses and minuses of working on your own. We'll discuss the personal motivation needed; we'll look at you as your own best resource; we'll see how another kind of network or support system—consisting of bankers, lawyers, and accountants—can make working on your own work for you. We'll look at the emotional price you pay for working on your own, how to preserve your image as a career woman if you work out of your bedroom or dining room, how to keep yourself from feeling isolated if you're a one-woman operation. We'll cover other practical aspects, from training courses and programs that can prepare you for setting up your own enterprise to how to set up a partnership.

As one of the many options open to career women, working on your own shouldn't be ignored. And although the climb up the corporate ladder may seem like heaven to you today, at some point you may want to pursue going into business for yourself, where the only boss you have to answer to is you.

Are You an Entrepreneurial Woman?

There have been many how-to books written on starting your own business. Most of them are chock-full of advice and personal experiences, and most of them take it for granted that if you are an entrepreneur, you're a man. The facts don't bear out the assumption. Many, many women work on their own in a variety of fields, from crafts to service companies to the creative arts, such as writing and painting, to fields like public relations and interior decorating. There are women with their own law or accounting firms. There are even women who own their own construction firms. The point is any business that a man can start a woman can start, too. That's point one in personal motivation for starting your own business. Feel free to survey the entire field of business because it's all open to you.

In *Up Your Own Organization!*, a handbook on how to start and finance a new business, author Donald M. Dible lists four elements that motivate a person to go into business for herself: the desire to be your own boss, the desire for fame, the desire for personal fortune, and the pure joy of winning.

Dible also lists several factors that make people leave corporations behind for their own enterprises. These are interesting, especially for just-blossoming career women who may want to use this list as a guide to whether corporations are making them happy or not. As Dible puts it, there are eight elements in the corporate experience "which provoke the enterpreneur to run screaming for the exit":

1. Inadequate corporate communications
2. Inequity between major contributions and financial rewards
3. Promotion and salary policies
4. Employment security
5. Corporate politics and nepotism
6. Red tape
7. Orphan products
8. Questionably relevant educational requirements

If most of these make you nod and smile bitterly, you may be closer than you think to striking out on your own. We've talked a lot about women being in control of their own lives. We've stressed this as an important value and approach to life. One sure-fire way to be totally in control of your business life is to go into business for yourself. Many women who have chosen this path have said they see it as an extension of their independence.

A literary agent who deals with both men and women clients says that her authors "love working at home. They have a flexibility that lets them use their time in the best way possible because no one else sets their priorities."

It's interesting that the four elements Dible lists center on independence, fame and recognition, wealth, and winning. As women become more and more independent, the desire to win becomes stronger, in the sense that they see risk as a challenge to their own abilities. As their confidence grows, taking a risk becomes more appealing because they feel they can succeed.

Also, as feminists have been saying for a decade, money is power, and the opportunity to make a lot of money can give women the sense of power that men have enjoyed for years.

As women gain more and more control of their own lives, the desire to do things "their way" becomes stronger and stronger. Working for yourself allows you to do things your way.

Of course, some careers, by their nature, require working on your own. A novelist or nonfiction writer, a painter, a poet, a sculptor need to work on their own. Some people whose work doesn't require them to work alone prefer its solitude and the flexibility. A woman author was quoted in a recent *New York Times* article as saying she preferred to work at home: "No one comes around with a coffee cart, breaking my trend of thought when I'm not the least bit hungry."

Whether it's a desire to do things your own way, get rich quick—or at least faster—earn greater recognition, or win in the business world, more and more women are choosing to work for themselves for the same reasons that men work for themselves, with one additional, highly significant factor playing a part in their decision. Some women work at home or in their own businesses in order to give themselves greater flexibility in rearing their children. Working at home means you can pursue your goals and still be there when your children need you. This is an advantage that has its disadvantages because unless you have full-time or part-time help or your children are in school, your physical presence will make them relate to you as mommy, not career woman. We'll talk more about how to deal with this problem through support systems later in this chapter.

Are You an Entrepreneurial Woman?

1. Do you enjoy taking risks?
2. Does challenge frighten you or exhilarate you?
3. Are you a self-starter who initiates activity, or are you more of a reactor?
4. Do you like to do things in your own way, on your own schedule?
5. How well do you deal with stress and pressure?
6. Do you enjoy working alone, or do you need others to bounce ideas off?
7. How good are you at structuring your own time?
8. Do you prefer giving or following orders?
9. Do you find the corporate structure exciting or confining?
10. Would you work long hours happily if the time were going into getting your own business started?

Gathering Your Resources to Start Your Own Business

Working at home and starting your own business are often two separate things. To avoid dealing with apples and oranges by combining the two, we'll deal with each one separately.

You've decided to set up your own business. Now what? Take the time to plan how your new enterprise is going to work.

When you make the decision to start your own business, the first thing you need to figure out, after you know what kind of business you're starting, is how much it will cost. What kind of capital and cash flow will you need for the first year? Do you have enough money of your own saved to start your business? If not, how will you finance it? You can go to a bank and get a small-business loan, or you can sell shares in your business to people who are willing to take a chance on your new venture. There are some principles to follow for both.

Banking is a serious business. Before you approach a bank for a small-business loan, have your proposal on paper, with realistic goals for what you expect to be the return on your investment.

Know what kind of capital outlay you'll have to make, and itemize it—for example, $10,000 for equipment (then list each piece of equipment and the cost), $30,000 for salaries for staff (and break that down into numbers of people and what you expect to pay each), rent, phone, ultilities, etc., anything that will be part of your operating costs. Ask to borrow the money you think you'll need, and make sure you've thought about how that money will be paid back every month. Do you have collateral for your loan? What will happen to you financially if your business fails? Would you be able to pay back the bank in any case?

You should have answers to all these questions before you approach a banker. The more you know about your business and goals, the more willing a bank will be to lend you the money.

If you are going to finance your new business by selling shares, you need a proposal and need to make some kind of guarantee of return on investment to your shareholders. We know of some people who have borrowed money from friends to start a new business, but they really didn't think ahead to how that money would be repaid. There were no set terms of repayment or the paying of dividends. In one case, when the business failed, the friends/shareholders lost their money. Although they lost cash, the woman entrepreneur who had approached them in the first place lost not only her money and theirs but some of her credibility when the venture failed. Part of her error was going to friends to invest in the first place. Business is business, and friendship is friendship. If you are taking a risk, it may be better not to risk your friends' money as well. Besides, friends like to help other friends, and they may not ask the tough business questions that other investors would. The best kinds of investors are the ones concerned about the bottom line. For one thing, they'll make sure you're concerned as well—and that's very important. When you're in business for yourself, profit had better be the name of the game, or you'll soon find yourself out of business.

Aside from a financial base, you need a sound physical and psychological base to go into business for yourself. In *Up Your Own Organization!*, Dible stresses that you'll never make it without what he calls the Three Ds: Desire, Determination, and Dedication. People who start their own businesses work long hours, often six or seven days a week when they're starting up—and they may not even have enough start-up capital to pay themselves salaries. In fact, in several of the case histories in *Up Your Own Organization!*, the owners and staffs of fledgling firms maintained full-time positions elsewhere while getting the new company started. They would work a forty-hour week for pay, then work another forty or fifty hours a week at the new venture, hoping that in time the new venture would be profitable enough that they could quit their full-time jobs and work full time for the new company. Unless you're willing to work long and hard at first, starting a new business is not for you.

Dible also stresses that you must be in excellent physical health because this kind of schedule puts extra strain on your body. And mentally you have to enjoy the challenge without getting ulcers over it.

Some people start new businesses in their own homes, using a den, bedroom, garage, even a dining-room table when the business is just beginning. Does your new venture lend itself to this kind of work space, or will you have to rent an office or some other kind of work space? You need to decide that in advance so that you can either convert or outfit a room at home or rent the necessary space.

Will you need a part-time or full-time staff for start-up? If you can use part-timers, often you can plug into people in the community—teenagers, senior citizens—whose hours are flexible and who are just dying to do something challenging and exciting, like helping you start a business.

If you're really going to go into business for yourself, you'll have to plug into yourself as a resource, using your own flexibility and creativity to make things happen. That all-important sense of humor will rescue you from feelings of hopelessness that often wash over people beginning a new enterprise.

One friend of ours, whose business literally began at the dining-room table, is now a successful jewelry designer who sells her original creations through chic boutiques and an ever-expanding mail-order business.

"But I never thought, when I started out, that it would really all work," she says. "I wanted desperately for it to succeed, but there were times when things seemed so grim. My little boy was in preschool, but he'd be home every afternoon, and there I'd be, trying to be supermom and get my designs drawn at the same time. Or I'd be making frantic calls to the factory where people were executing my designs, worrying that an order wouldn't be ready in time. For the first year I don't think we ever entertained in the dining room. My work just filled the whole room, from the table to every available surface. Luckily my husband has a sense of humor, and he believed in my designs. He knew it was only a matter of time until I could move out of the dining room forever."

Today she has her own studio and two junior associates helping with the design work.

If you're married and have a family, being successful at starting your own business will mean having the support of your husband and children. If you're going to work long hours, risk some of the family's accumulated capital, and possibly take over part of the house, it will have to be a family project, or your life will be in constant turmoil. You'll need your family as a support system more than ever.

Finally, you'll need what we call the entrepreneurial woman's support system: a lawyer, an accountant, and a banker. You need a lawyer to help you incorporate or form a company, to check out zoning laws if you're opening a business, to make sure any agreements or contracts you sign are not only legal but in your best interest. Lawyers are used to reading the fine print and translating legalese into plain English. Get recommendations from other businessmen and women on whom they use, then meet with several lawyers before deciding who will be your legal counsel. Make sure whoever you use is willing to explain to you every action he or she takes on your behalf. Of course, you should trust him, but you should also understand his reasons for doing things.

You'll need an accountant and possibly a bookkeeper, depending on the complexity and size of your business, to keep your finances in order. Preferably find an accountant whom you can use for personal and business financial matters, especially if he or she is the person who will be doing your income taxes; that way, he will be able to tell you which are personal and which are business deductions. Tax laws are complex; he will be able to wade through the verbiage and make sure you get any deductions that are coming to you.

In the *New York Times* of July 15, 1979, an article on working at home pointed out some tax advantages:

> . . . The tax savings can be considerable for the home worker. The Internal Revenue Service allows deductions for portions of the home used exclusively and "regularly" for business purposes and either as the principal place of business, or as the place where clients or customers are normally seen. Deductions for expenses related to the maintenance and operation of the area are allowed as well: depreciation, rent, utilities, insurance and, in some cases, mortgage interest and real estate taxes.

You need a good accountant to make you aware of all these deductions and to organize the financial end of your business so that it operates on a cost-efficient basis. In *Up Your Own Organization!*, author Donald M. Dible states that the main reason for small business failure is inefficient—or incompetent—management. If you have the right experts helping you, you'll increase your chances of success.

You need a banker with whom you can establish and maintain an ongoing business relationship. The man—or woman—you go to for your first business loan can be the person you approach for your expansion loan. Bankers are experts in their area, and you should form an ongoing relationship, not only for financial help as you need it but to gather some of that knowledge that bankers have and are generally only too willing to share with an interested—and informed—consumer, especially one who is—or potentially will be—a big customer.

If You Go into Partnership

Some people who go into business for themselves prefer to share the burdens and the rewards with another person in a partnership. There are advantages and disadvantages.

Advantages: You make half the investment, take half the risk, work half as many hours, and solve half as many problems than if you tackled the job on your own.

Disadvantages: You must share decisions, income, and recognition, and you must adjust or accommodate to someone else's style of working and doing business.

The key to succeeding in a partnership is to choose your partner carefully. Either choose a "soul mate" who is as close as you can get to a mirror image of you in style, approach, and talents, or choose someone with complementary attitudes and skills, so that she is strong where you're weak, and vice versa. For example, if you have the creative talent, you might choose a partner with a strong business sense. If you are shy with people and you need to sell your product or services, you might choose a partner who is good with people and has highly developed selling skills.

Temperamentally you can be alike or different, but if you're different, again your temperaments need to complement each other if the partnership is to work. For example, you may be impulsive, able to make quick decisions. Often you're right, but sometimes you rush too quickly into things. Your partner may be slower to come to a decision but may analyze the problem more carefully before deciding. By joining forces, you've created your own system of checks and balances—you press her when you need to act and she's slow to move; she slows you down when a deal needs a second look.

Whether your talents, attitudes, approaches, and temperaments are the same or different, you need to like, trust, and respect each other. In a way a partnership is like a business marriage. Unless there is a positive, strong core, it will fall apart during stressful times. And when you're beginning a new business, there's bound to be a lot of stress.

When we talked about going into business for yourself, we mentioned the need for good physical and mental health. This is just as critical with partners. Physically you both need to be in top shape to share the rigors of starting a business. Mentally each of you needs to be strong, resourceful, independent, and self-confident, or one will become either a threat or a crutch to the other. An ideal partnership functions like a matched team of horses.

You need open communication and honesty between you to come to decisions and resolve—quickly—any differences that occur between you. If one or both of you sulk, carry grudges or need to get revenge, the partnership will blow up in your faces, and the business will probably go right along with it.

Aside from a good personal relationship, you need an objective, binding legal contract that spells out the rights and responsibilities for each of you. Legitimate disagreements can occur and contractual disputes happen every day. An objective, written contract protects the rights of both of you and spells out the rules of the game so that they are clear to both parties.

Once the groundwork has been laid, you will need large doses of flexibility and a sense of humor. You'll be working closely together, and the day-in, day-out closeness may begin to fray your nerves unless you can compromise or laugh about the bad times.

Getting Organized to Work at Home

When you work at home, you have to be disciplined. After all, there's no office to go to, no one else's routine to follow, no one else's expectations to meet. You've got to be a self-starter, and you need to have your place of work at home clearly defined and organized. Ideally you'll have a separate room to work in. It not only gives you the necessary physical space for files, desk, chair, etc. but gives you a psychic lift as well. As you walk into your "office" each morning, your workday has officially begun. If you use a makeshift work area, you place an extra burden on yourself: setting up and dismantling your work site every day. It may work short term, but long term, not only is it inefficient, but it will drive you crazy.

When you set up your own space, equip it with everything you'll need, right at your fingertips. It's best to have a separate business phone if you can, and heaven is a tape machine or answering service so that the calls that get through are the necessary, work-related ones, while the time-wasting ones are filtered out.

A writer we know who worked at home said she couldn't function until she got an answering machine for her phone. "Between my mother, my friends, my husband, and various over-the-phone solicitations, I would barely get started when the phone would interrupt me. After two weeks of frustration I installed an answering machine. Now I can work uninterruptedly, returning calls when my workday is done. I have a special business phone for the important calls I must take, from my agent, the editors I deal with, and a few select others."

We did an informal survey of the women we know who work at home and found that all of them structured their days with a routine, so that work actually got done. Even if you're single, with no children to make demands on your time, unless you've disciplined yourself into a routine, you can waste a lot of time doing nonessential chores around the house, reading, watching television, or talking on the phone, telling yourself you'll get to the work "later." Two things happen when you go through this syndrome: You work inefficiently, and you feel a constant, nagging guilt that you haven't accomplished what you set out to do. A routine structures your work time, allowing you to labor efficiently and to walk away from your work without guilt once you've accomplished the day's tasks. You can apply your time management techniques to organize your day into segments of work and leisure time. That way you can take full advantage of your flexibility without cutting down on your efficiency.

One man we know actually showers, shaves, and dresses for business every morning before going into his "home office." He takes his coffee into his "office" and begins his workday punctually at nine and ends it punctually at five. Since he is an insurance broker, these hours work beautifully for him, and he told us that psychologically, getting dressed for work sets his routine in motion each day.

Be flexible. Use whatever technique works for you. A writer we know plays all day and works most of the night. Since he lives alone, his odd work hours don't bother anyone else, and he couldn't be happier with the arrangement. He finds his peak productive time is between 10:00 P.M. and 4:00 A.M. Evaluate your own body clock, and set your hours accordingly. Of course, if your business depends on working with others, you may have to schedule some of your work time during the nine-to-five hours, but even then you can build in flexibility with a ten-to-six work schedule, or eight-to-four or eleven-to-seven. One of the things employees in corporations complain of when asked what causes them stress on their jobs is the regimentation, the routine of their days. When you work on your own, you can beat the system by building in your own flexibility. Just remember that even flexibility takes thought and planning.

The Price You Pay for Working on Your Own

As you know by now, we feel that whatever options you choose in life, you pay to play. Working on your own is no exception. For all the benefits and psychic rewards, there are problems and trade-offs.

For one thing, if you're the kind of person who needs the structure and order of an office routine, you will either have to forego working on your own or have to establish your own routine that you pursue without fail. We know one woman who worked in public relations for fifteen years before retiring with her husband to the country to write books. She had always had more energy than most, cranking out press releases, planning press events and parties, making presentations to reporters and editors. But a funny thing happened to her drive when she left the corporate environment: She felt as if her motor had stopped, and it took her more than a year to adjust to being an initiator of activity, rather than a reactor. For fifteen years she had met other people's deadlines, needs, and requirements. She had written only what she had been told to write about and only in the prescribed way. Left suddenly on her own to schedule her time, to choose her activities and the subject matter of the books she planned to write, she felt very uneasy. And tired. Suddenly she had lost her pep.

"I finally figured out that I really thrive on structure," she told us. "I had always fantasized about having my time all to myself, but once I got what I thought I wanted, I realized either I'd have to build some of my own structure into my work schedule, or I'd never write a book."

She decided to divide her time between writing books and doing community public relations, on a volunteer basis, in the small town in which she lives. The public relations events and press releases give her a sense of structure against which she could use her "free time" to write her books.

In Chapter Two we talked about the importance of knowing yourself. When you work on your own, this becomes even more necessary because there are no other people to distract you from focusing on you, no one else to blame if the work doesn't get done.

Another problem with working at home is the sense of isolation many women feel, especially at first. If you've just made the transition from a business or corporate environment to working within your own four walls, it can suddenly seem too quiet, too dull; you may feel that the friends you made through work will forget you because you're no longer on the scene. You may get depressed during the first week or the first month if you find yourself working through the day without the customary break and camaraderie of the business lunch or lunch with friends. You may even miss the people contact of getting out and commuting to work every day. You may feel left out of the hustle and bustle of life.

But wait. Before you decide to abandon your dream of working at home because you couldn't bear the loneliness we've just described, read on. The women we know who work at home have found solutions to these feelings of isolation and loneliness, and they had to look no farther than their own resourcefulness and initiative.

Rebecca, who writes at home, has lunch at least two days a week with various friends who work in nearby suburban communities. She prefers not to meet friends for lunch every day, but she knows she needs those two days of friendly lunches to feel that she's in the mainstream of life. She also jogs three miles every morning with her husband, an activity she says invigorates her for the rest of the day and, equally important, gets her up and out early each morning. She eats breakfast with her daughter, then settles in to work. On the days when she doesn't lunch out, she works straight through until her daughter returns from school. They spend some time together, compare notes on their days, and Rebecca begins to make the transition between her workday and her leisure time with her family. Evenings are spent with her daughter and her husband, Sam. So much for her sense of isolation.

Lucy, an interior decorator who works out of her home, gets more than enough people contact each day dealing with her clients. Most days she's too busy to lunch with friends, but she catches up with them over dinner once a week. In her leisure time she's active in the women's movement on a volunteer basis, helping other women reenter the work force.

When we asked her if she ever felt isolated or lonely, she laughed. "My only problem is the days aren't long enough to do everything I want to do, see my friends, and be as active as I'd like in helping other women find careers. The only time I ever felt lonely was fifteen years ago, when my husband and I divorced and I was left at home with two young children. Once I began my decorating business, the loneliness vanished. I discovered I'd been only as lonely as I'd allowed myself to be, sitting at home, embarrassed, in a way, that my marriage had failed in a suburban community of couples. Once I realized that I could make it on my own, that I was intersting and valuable on my own, I had as many friends and activities as I needed."

The key is to know how much contact with people you need and to build that into your daily routine. Just because you're working at home doesn't mean you have to shut yourself away from other people and events.

Ellen, a free-lance artist who lives in New York City, loves to explore her neighborhood and adjacent ones on the "walking tours" she takes once or twice a week. "I find I just like being out among people; I don't necessarily have to be with them all the time. I've discovered lots of little shops, some charming older buildings, some quaint neighborhoods, and I've become an inveterate people watcher. And I'll tell you something else. The observations I make on my walking tours help me in my work. I sometimes find myself drawing a building I've seen or a person I've seen into the illustrations I do."

Annabelle, a psychologist who practices at home, has two passions in life besides her work and her husband: tennis and movies. "I take a tennis lesson every week and play at least two or three times a week—during the day, when it's a lot easier to get court time. I'm a good tennis player and getting better all the time, plus I feel the exercise I get is great for my body and my mind—it's very refreshing. I see patients one evening a week, but I take an afternoon off to compensate for that extra time, and on that one afternoon a week I go to the movies. Alone. Living in New York, I used to find it difficult to see all the movies I wanted to see because there were always long lines at night for the best movies. By seeing them in the afternoon, I get in without a wait. I'm totally current on the latest films. I save the ones I know my husband wants to see for an evening or weekend, but that still leaves me lots of movies for my weekly film watching."

The ways people solve the problem of isolation are as varied as their careers and their interests in life. The point is, the mere fact of working at home needn't isolate you.

The flip side of the isolation problem is the constant interruptions problem. We've already talked about having a separate business phone and letting a tape machine or answering service take all personal calls when you're working. But friends, neighbors, and family can be a source of interruption if they make unannounced visits. This seems to happen more in the suburbs and in small towns, where visiting is more casual and spontaneous than in major urban areas and where fewer women work all day.

A free-lance writer living in the Middle West told us that neighbors would regularly drop by to chat over coffee when she first moved to the area eight years ago.

"I wanted to be accepted, to have them like me, and I didn't want them to think I was a snob, so for a couple of months I never said anything when they'd drop in in the morning or afternoon just to 'talk.' I told them all that I was a writer, but it didn't seem to penetrate that a writer needs time to write. After two months my need to write overcame my desire to be accepted. I told them all, politely but firmly, that I write from nine in the morning until three in the afternoon, when the kids come home from school. I said I'd be happy to see them, but we'd have to schedule the time. I must say a couple of those women stopped being my friends. But the two or three women I really liked understood and asked· me why I hadn't told them sooner that they were interrupting my writing time. I still see them a lot, eight years later, but never between nine and three. Even though my kids are grown now, I've stuck to the same writing routine, and they respect it."

No one can work effectively with a thousand interruptions. Friends and family need to be told that you're working. The fact that you're working at home makes no difference.

In the transition from working in an office to working at home, some married women come up against the problem of husbands who now see them, at some level, as homemakers. They begin assigning chores and errands, prefacing each request with "Since you're at home . . ."

"You need to cut them off at the pass," one woman artist told us. "The first time my husband suggested I do all the errands we usually do together on Saturday, I just said no, explaining to him that I would be working just as hard at home as he would be at his office. He persisted for a while until we started getting the money from the handmade Christmas ornaments I design. He'd always thought they were cute, but he'd had no idea they'd be so lucrative. The cash coming in really got his attention, and he's never suggested again that I run his errands. After all, my time is money."

You just can't indulge a husband's fantasy that you're now the little woman working at home. As we've said before, most people feel the need at some time to have a "wife" in the traditional sense of the word: someone to nurture and care for them, to take care of their every need, with never a thought to their own. But realistically, if you have a career and it's not homemaking, you don't have the time, energy, or inclination to be a wife in that sense. And your husband wouldn't want to fill that role either.

So much for the problems with husband, friends, and family—all adults who, after a little persuasion or some downright rudeness, will get the message that you are working. Do not disturb. But what about children? If you have preschoolers and you've suddenly stopped going to the office to work at home, they're going to be confused for a while. Our advice: Whatever child care arrangements you had while working at the office should remain in effect. Whether you had part-time or full-time help or some kind of day care or preschool facility, don't give it up to become full-time mommy if you really plan to work at home. You'll have too many distractions from people too young to understand that you're physically there but not available to them at every minute. With help, your children can observe mommy at work, see her more often than they did when she worked away from home, but won't keep you from working.

If this sounds cold, consider the alternative. You want to work, and you decide to work at home. But your young child or children prevent you from doing this. It would be natural for you to feel guilt if you ignored them and resentment if you sacrificed your work to their every need. They would sense your guilt and play on it, and they would sense your resentment and feel hurt. You just can't send contradictory messages to your children and expect them to understand. And you can't cut yourself in two and expect to be effective in either role you've chosen for yourself.

That leads us to another problem of working at home: your image. For many people, at home is at home. Work is something

you do at a factory or office. Merely announcing that you're
working at home won't change the image for some people. It will
take time and repeated words and actions on your part to convey
the new you, a serious career person whose place of work happens
to be her home. You're not just puttering around or taking up a
hobby; you're doing productive work. The more people see you
as a professional, the more they will treat you like one. This is
especially important if you're dealing with clients.

If your office is in your home and you see clients there, your
office should look like an office, even if it's only one room. It
should be neat and businesslike, and so should you. If a client appears in his or her business suit, attaché case in hand, you shouldn't
greet him or her at the door in your jeans and T-shirt. Your image
has just been blown. If you have children, they shouldn't be running in and out of your office, wanting to play, when you're meeting with a client. People may say to your face that it's cute or
charming, but they will go away wondering how professional you
are, how serious you are about what you do. Your sense of organization should be obvious to your client. Relevant papers should be
properly filed and readily available. This is not a problem that
applies only to people who work at home; many people who work
in offices have cluttered desks and piles of papers that give the
impression of chaos (and often is). But creating a businesslike impression is even more important when you work at home.

On the other hand, you can use the advantages of working at
home to enhance your image. If you have a lovely breakfast room
or dining room, you can meet clients over breakfast or lunch, prepared in advance and not served by you, even if you have to hire
a neighborhood teenager to do the honors. This way you stress the
elegant informality of your lifestyle, which can be a refreshing
change for a harried business person used to meeting in offices and
boardrooms. By being organized and dignified in the preparation
and serving of a meal or refreshments, you make yourself a con-
genial hostess rather than a super schlepper who is cooking while
she's working.

Image is important and gets results. If you're in doubt, take a look at our public figures, from rock stars to presidents. All of them establish images and build on them through the way they dress, speak, live, behave. Even con artists can be used as a role model, in one sense. If you observe the way they operate, they usually follow the principle of the bigger the con, the bigger the front. They will even rent plush offices and hire personnel to project an affluent image in order to gain the trust and confidence of the people they want to defraud. Of course, you're dealing not in fraud, but in genuine values exchanged. Still, the image you project can very well determine whether you get the business or not.

In a *New York Times* article on working at home, a major negative of doing so was that "Psychologically, there's no real separation between professional and private life." That is a very real problem for some people, especially those who tend to be compulsive or verge on being workaholics. It may sound paradoxical, but the only solution to that particular problem is self-discipline. We're used to thinking of using self-discipline to get ourselves to work, but it is every bit as valuable in getting us to stop working when it is time to quit.

Anyone who has a career will go through times when extra hours must be spent to meet a deadline, and that's perfectly okay. But if, day after day, you find you can't leave your work alone, especially since it's right there waiting for you in the next room, you're going to have to put on the mental brakes. Slow down, and think it through. If you've made a work schedule for yourself and you're accomplishing the goals you've set for yourself each day, there is no need to feel chained to your desk, unable to enjoy leisure time.

Because you work at home, there is no physical separation between work and your private life; this means you have to set up a mental separation, in your own mind, that allows you to shift your gears away from work and into your private life. The principle is the same whether you work at home or in an office. When you work at home, you just have to use your imagination more in going from work to pleasure. If you can't trust yourself to stick to your schedule and quit work at a reasonable time, make plans for the end of the day that commit you to activities with others. You may have to leave home for a period of time—either for a short walk, dinner, or a movie out—to create the barrier you need to separate your work from your private life. If you have this problem, use whatever technique works for you, but make sure you don't turn something you love—your work—into an escape from or an avoidance of the rest of your life.

Can I Afford to Work for Myself?

This is a question only you can answer. We've already talked about start-up capital, financing, and overhead, but we haven't dealt with some hidden aspects. First of all, will you be able to make as much initially, working for yourself, as you did when you worked for someone else? If you can't, can you afford a self-imposed cut in income, or can you take on a part-time or second job to tide you over until your business pays off? If you're married, is your husband willing to subsidize your enterprise, and can he afford to do so? If you're married, going into business on your own can never be a unilateral decision since it affects another person's life. Will the money you save on work clothes, commuting, and daily lunches out in any way compensate for the projected loss in income?

Of course, no one can ever be sure how much she will make in a new enterprise. On the other hand, you need to research as carefully as you can the potential return on your investment of time, effort, and money. And you need to estimate pretty accurately how long it will take to get that return.

If you're single and your own sole means of support, you'll need a cushion in savings of at least six months' salary; some experts say, with the current rate of inflation, it should be nine months' salary. You'll also need medical, life, and home insurance. Do you have it, and can you afford it? No one lives her life waiting for a crisis to occur; on the other hand, you need to be prepared for crises that can occur. If you're running a one-person business and become ill, your income will cease. If you've invested all you have in a business and it fails, how will you eat?

You need to ask yourself all these questions before you make the final decision to strike out on your own. Use the network for entrepreneurial women we talked about earlier in this chapter to get a true reading on your financial picture from your accountant, to get advice on financing and savings options from your banker, and to get any legal advice on insurance and liability from your lawyer.

Tapping into Yourself as a Creative Resource

You've been reading this chapter, and suddenly you think, "I'd like to work for myself, but what can I do on my own?" We advise you to tap into yourself as a creative resource. You may be a writer, an artist, a designer. You may be a real estate broker, an insurance broker, a public relations consultant, a doctor, a lawyer, an accountant, a psychologist. You may be an employment counselor, an executive recruiter, a literary or talent agent. You may be a shoemaker, a weaver, a jewelry designer, a cook, or a chef. Almost every profession, trade, service, or occupation allows you the freedom to work for yourself. Even in smaller communities, the range of entrepreneurial endeavors is vast. For example, in Akron, Joyce knew people in the community self-employed in the following ways: One bought and sold tires and trucking equipment; another ran a home improvement business; another did house and interior painting and bought, refurbished, and sold antiques. She knew several doctors, dentists, and lawyers, several families in the restaurant business, a score of hairdressers, two women who owned a boutique that sold only stylish maternity clothes, a fellow who made hand-crafted furniture from petrified redwood . . . the list could go on and on.

When you work for yourself, you can create your own job, fill an existing need, provide a necessary service or introduce something new into the marketplace. One of the best success stories we heard was of a man who, in a sense, followed the Pet Rock lead.

(You remember the Pet Rock, merchandised at Christmas several years ago as the no-care pet? It seemed ridiculous but appealed to people's sense of whimsy and ended up being a million-dollar seller.) The man we remember is the one who created and merchandised the Executive Teddy Bear as a gift item for Christmas 1977. Here was a man who saw a need and filled it. He had read all the stories about harried middle-management types and corporate stress. He had heard them complain that no one understood them or gave them recognition. And he came up with a solution. He created the Executive Teddy Bear, a cuddly stuffed bear which, when you pulled a string, would say warm and encouraging things like "You're doing a great job." In a story which appeared in the *Chicago Tribune* in 1977, the man was amazed with his own success. He had completely sold out his existing stock and had a backlog of orders. We recently saw an ad again for the Executive Teddy Bear and assume he is still going strong.

The point of the story is that the range of merchandisable products, goods, and services is limited only by your own imagination and talents. Don't disregard whimsy. Let your creative juices flow. After all, somewhere, chuckling, is the man who invented the Hula-Hoop, followed by the man who made a million with a bar of bath soap in the shape of a microphone which appealed to all those people who sing in the shower, not to mention the long-dead ancient who first thought of backgammon or the Philadelphia engineer who spent his summers in Atlantic City and devised a board game to immortalize its streets in Monopoly.

If you've got the entrepreneurial spirit, the whole world is open to you. And if the risk and the challenge make you laugh rather than cry, working for yourself can be one of the most rewarding ways to have it all.

Getting Help in Striking Out on Your Own

Becoming a successful businesswoman is an acquired art. You don't have to know it all to strike out on your own; there are people who can help you.

Largely as a result of the women's movement, major institutions, from the government to banks to colleges and universities, have become responsive to the needs of women. All these institutions have information and, in some cases, financial aid or special programs that can help you. Part of having it all is being open to learning all your life. You should never pass up the opportunity to learn from others' expertise or to take advantage of the benefits available to you.

Almost every college and university has courses in accounting, bookkeeping, financial planning, and management. If your idea of how the financial end of a business should work is sketchy, take one of these courses. Check the guidance office of the school to find out whether there is a course specially tailored for entrepreneurs. If there isn't, ask its advice on the best course for your needs.

Aside from colleges and universities, organizations like the YWCA run programs, workshops, and seminars geared to women who are seeking careers. They run the gamut from assertiveness training—you'll need to be assertive to make your own way in the marketplace—to reentry and career counseling to management skills. Other women's groups and, increasingly, business groups of both sexes sponsor seminars on management skills and how to start (or how to run more effectively) your own business. Check into the availability of these in your community.

The federal government has become increasingly interested in careers for women as women have become more involved in the political process. For example, there are special loans available to women who want to start their own businesses. Find out what is available to you from the government on all levels, from local to federal. Often funds go unused because people don't know they exist.

Increasingly banks are sponsoring seminars on money management. See if one of these applies to a woman in her own business. If you are currently working in a profession and want to branch out on your own, check out whether your own professional organization has programs or seminars in how to start your own business in your field of expertise.

Your women's network will help you here as well. Talk to all the women you know who've started their own businesses. Learn from their experiences, good and bad. They may very well help you to avoid pitfalls that hurt or hindered them.

Starting your own business is a complex enterprise. Get as much input as you can from people with expertise in any area you need to know more about. Most people are flattered at your interest in them, and if you don't personally know any women in your field who are in business for themselves, check the phone book or the latest edition of *Who's Who in American Women* to compile a list of women you might call and interview. The most successful people tend to be the most generous with their time and advice. If they're willing to see you or talk with you over the phone, carefully prepare a list of all the questions you want to ask them. You'll end up not only with advice but with a potential network of women doing the same thing you are, who can help and advise each other in the coming years.

SEVEN

WHEN IT COMES TIME TO *UNDERSTAND* MONEY

We live close to the wire. We spend just about everything we make. We try to save, to plan ahead, but somehow, what with inflation and the high cost of living, we never seem to have enough to go around, although we both make a substantial income. I know we should make our money work for us, but it seems neither of us has the knack.

I'm always on top of money. It's very important because it means freedom, the ability to manage your own life. Money makes you independent. I have always budgeted and managed savings. I've always been on the cheap side—I've taken subways and buses instead of cabs. It works for me. I don't like credit cards, and I don't use them—only for business. I've always carried a minimal amount of cash to control spending.

I'm in a transitional stage with managing money. I'm getting much better. I feel now that I'm getting on top of it, but that wasn't always the case. I save as much as I can, but most of that goes to pay my son's school tuition. Money is still something I have to worry about, to track very carefully, or I'd have a problem.

MONEY CAN MEAN power, a tool that can work for you, if you understand it. Yet, even though more than half the women in America are working outside the home, many of them still don't understand how money works. (In fairness, many men don't either. An article that appeared in the *Wall Street Journal* focused on the large percentage of men and women earning above $35,000 who have filed for bankruptcy.)

Although some men have the same problems with money that many women have, women are more likely to experience them because of a lack of familiarity with controlling money. Men are encouraged to understand money; women are encouraged to find a man who understands money.

The result: You see women who are successful in their careers, who can tackle any project and win, yet don't understand how to enjoy their money and be comfortable with it. The women we interviewed fell into two classes: those who really felt money controlled them and didn't have any plan for managing it and those who felt they had money under control through budgeting and saving. Not one of the women we spoke to treated money as a tool for gaining increased power. Not one of them, the authors included, saw investment as something they were totally comfortable with.

Yet we all know that no one gets rich working for someone else. We all know that money—enough of it—is the key to independence, to buying personal options, from a house in the country to a sabbatical from work to the best education for our children.

This chapter is going to outline the effects money can and does have on our lifestyles. We need to put as much energy and drive into gaining control of our finances as we put into other areas of our lives. Whether your husband, father, lover, or brother understands money isn't relevant. It's whether *you* understand it that counts. Just as you wouldn't allow anyone else to take charge of any other major area of your life, you wouldn't want to allow anyone to take charge of your money. Money is a means of having it all. The sooner you start thinking of it that way, the better.

We've put together a guide for determining what kind of money manager you are. There are basically four types. You may fit into one category or be a combination of two or three or even all four. Be honest in evaluating your own money management skills. After all, the point of this chapter is to provide principles that will help you gain control of your money and stay in control of it. Remember, money buys options, and we don't want you to be shortchanged.

Begin by asking yourself this basic question: If I could handle my money any way I wanted to, how would I handle it?

Would you handle it yourself, feeling totally in control by knowing where every penny went and budgeting to the last dime?

Would you throw caution to the wind and never pay any attention to where the money went until one day your banker—or your creditors—told you that there was a problem?

Would you like to understand the mechanics of good money management but leave the day-to-day hassles of budgeting and paying bills to someone else?

Once you understand what category of money manager you

fit into, what really makes you satisfied with your financial affairs, you can begin to gain control.

Category I: The Inner-Controlled Money Manager

If she's married, she manages the money for the family. She is almost compulsive about knowing where every dollar goes, and she plans carefully. She saves. She rarely borrows except for major purchases or emergencies. She has a clear idea of what credit is all about but hesitates to use it although it may be to her advantage in an economy that demands the manipulation of credit to the consumer's advantage.

Somewhere in her childhood she was imbued with the Protestant work ethic that only through hard work can one ever achieve financial security, and financial security is a key issue in her life. She feels that no one else could ever understand and manage her finances as well as she does.

The Problems: She has fallen into the "can't see the forest for the trees" trap. Although she feels she's totally in control of her money, she may not be managing it to her greatest advantage. She works hard, but she doesn't work smart, and she never lets her money work for her. She can drive the people around her crazy with her compulsive money management techniques, wasting valuable time chasing down every penny and driving away husband and friends with her desire to be totally in control of every cent.

Prognosis: If you recognize yourself in this description, you need to relax your rigid policies. If you haven't already driven off your husband or lover, begin to bend a little. Involve him in the management of your joint funds. Ask his opinion and advice. You may decide that you want to seek the professional expertise of a tax consultant or money manager if your joint income is in the $50,000 or above income range. Or you may want to take a money management course to learn more efficient and profitable money management techniques. Consult your colleagues in the Old Girls' Network to find out how other career women deal with money matters. Finally, remember that the fact that your checkbook balances and you stay within your budget doesn't make you a smart manager of money.

Category II: The Scarlet O'Hara "I'll Think About It Tomorrow" Money Manager

It's more than likely that this kind of woman was brought up to believe that money is a dirty word, best left to the men to worry about. Whenever she has money problems, she puts her head in the sand and hopes they go away. If she's married, it's guaranteed that her husband manages the money and that he is her financial warden, telling her how much money she can spend. Of course, she usually overspends and then gets angry if he tells her so. After all, she's earning a good income, too, and money is just something that women spend without thinking about it.

If she's single, she writes checks and crosses her fingers, hoping there is enough money in her account to cover them, since she never balances her checkbook and has no idea what's actually in her account, except that she knows it's never much. If she comes from a wealthy or comfortable family, she depends on her mother, her father, her brother, or her rich uncle to bail her out if she's seriously in debt. She thinks of it as a loan because she always intends to pay it back. Of course, she never does. If there's no one to bail her out, she just goes merrily on her way, worrying a bit more when the bills come in but never dwelling on her financial problems and never taking any action to change her attitudes toward money management.

The Problems: The dangers are obvious; only the degree of indebtedness will vary. If you don't mind being constantly in debt and having no financial cushion to fall back on, you just may survive. But you're really vulnerable to any change in financial fortunes because as a money manager you are totally out of control. If some man doesn't come along to take care of you, you may very well find yourself poverty-stricken in your old age, with nothing to fall back on.

Prognosis: If you fit the description and are willing to admit it, you may be ready to take the first step toward gaining control of your money. But old habits die hard, so you'll have to really discipline yourself to get control of your finances. If you're not committed, forget it. If you are committed, you can follow one of two paths: You can take a course on money management and read several books that will give you guidance on how to manage your money properly, or you can decide to use a professional financial manager who will balance your checkbook, pay your bills, and tell you how much you can spend without getting into trouble.

Category III: The Outer-Controlled Money Manager

She is smart enough to realize that she doesn't understand how to manage her money effectively, so since she wants to be in control of it, she has an outside expert handle it for her. She may use a tax accountant or a professional money manager. She realizes that like most women, she was not brought up to think that money management would be her responsibility and, therefore, never bothered to learn about it. But she was shrewd enough to know how to shore up her weakness by hiring outside strength.

The Problems: While she is certainly more in control of her money than the Scarlett O'Hara type, she can get into trouble if she delegates all financial responsibility without understanding the basics of sound money management. If she doesn't understand the basics, she will have trouble telling a good from a bad money manager. And a bad one can get her into every bit as much trouble as she could get into herself. Because she lacks the awareness of how to manage her money effectively, she could very well miss a good opportunity to get a greater return on her money, even if it's staring her in the face.

Prognosis: If you fit this description, you don't have major problems. You can eliminate having any problems by learning enough to know how money ought to be managed and by choosing carefully a professional money manager. He or she should be given greater and greater responsibility for your financial affairs gradually, as you see positive results and begin to trust that he or she will do the right thing with your money. After all, it's your money, so you'll want to be ultimately in control. And you can't be in control of your money without understanding it.

Category IV: The Hybrid
She is a combination of the first three types, someone who may know that eventually she'd like someone else to manage her money more effectively but who hasn't reachd that stage yet. In the meantime, she's realistic enough about her finances to keep herself out of any major trouble, taking whatever steps she needs to in order to survive.

The Problems: Because the hybrid is a combination of two or three types, her problems can vary according to which type dominates. She really needs to identify all the "money personalities" she has and determine which personality is in control most of the time. Then she can analyze whether her problems are major or minor, long-term or short-term. If she finds herself mostly in the Scarlett O'Hara camp, she should get a money manager or at least some financial counseling right away to avoid large debts or even bankruptcy.

Prognosis: Since the hybrid wants ultimately to be in control of her money, time will solve most of her problems. All she really needs to know is what she needs to learn about money management and how soon she needs to learn it. If she's doing fairly well on her own, with a commonsense approach, she can wait until she can afford an outside expert. If she finds herself stumbling and about to fall, she needs to get help fast.

Once you've identified what type of money manager you are, you can take the necessary steps to gain full control of your money.

Avoid Living Beyond Your Income

When they've worked hard and long, it's difficult for some people not to spend it when they suddenly find themselves making "big money." Of course, big money is a relative term—it can be

$10,000 for one person, $50,000 for another—but the feeling is the same: Now that I have it, I want to spend it.

One friend, thinking back over her life, told us, "Remember the good old days, when we didn't know the difference between a Timex and a Cartier Tank watch? When our bookcases were bricks and boards and we got excited when we could afford a real stereo set?" She sighed. "It's all so different now. Back then I didn't know how much there was to want. Now that I know, I seem to want everything. And I want it right this minute. I want all the trappings of success. All the right things."

We understood what she was saying. Status seeking is a trap all its own. So is having everything right now. And keeping up with the Joneses. One woman complained to us, "Last year was the year of the fur coat at my company. It seemed everyone—even the secretaries—had one. I hadn't even thought about a fur coat before, but by the middle of the winter it was the only thing I wanted. And it seemed that it said something about me, that I didn't have one—that I couldn't afford one. I managed to resist—it wasn't something I really wanted, and my husband and I had other priorities. But I know this year there will be something else that I'll have to resist."

For some people, the more they get, the more they want. For themselves. To impress their friends and family. To reassure themselves they're successful. Wanting things and acquiring them aren't bad, but losing control over your acquisitive appetite can be financial—and psychological—disaster.

A guiding principle of having it all is knowing what's most important to you and going after it. Since many of the things that are most important are material things, they need to be planned and budgeted. We all have daydreams of what we'd do with a million dollars if it fell into our hands, but those are daydreams, not reality, at least for the moment. For the moment our incomes, large or small, are what we have to work with. And income can be divided only so many ways. If all of it is on your back or in your house or apartment, there is no money for the unexpected—good or bad.

We know of one man who started his own company and is now

enjoying its success. He had only one regret in the way he started his business. He had had to borrow the start-up capital of $500 because he hadn't saved a dime of his salary. He had almost missed the business opportunity of his life by not having the money to invest in it.

When you live up to or beyond your income, you limit your options. In an increasingly credit-oriented society, it is easy to rack up debts without even realizing it. The charges revolve, accruing interest, which you must pay, while you pay the minimum amount monthly until one day you wake up and a large part of your income is going to pay for what you already have—with interest.

Susan has one solution to that particular problem. She uses credit cards only for business. If she can't pay cash, she doesn't buy. Cindy is more comfortable with credit and uses it, rather than lets it use her. "I'll use my credit cards and then pay the bill in full within the thirty-day period. That way I accomplish two things: I get to use the credit free, without paying interest, and I get to use the credit free, without paying interest, and I get more for my money since, with the rate of inflation, the credit extended to me at the beginning of the month is worth more in actual dollar value than the money I pay at the end of the month."

Whatever way you choose to deal with credit, be sure you understand it before you indulge in credit buying. Pay close attention to the *terms* of the credit agreement, so that you know how to make the best use of the credit extended to you. The same is true of loans—for cars, a mortgage for a house, a personal loan. The terms of interest and repayment are more critical than the amount borrowed.

Budgeting is crucial to staying within your income. Even the women we talked to who said they didn't budget wished they did. It's really the only way to be in control of your money because you have a plan. You know where the dollars are supposed to go, and if something doesn't add up at the end of each month or each quarter, you can see where your projections were off or where you just plain overspent.

Impulse buying is another trap to avoid if you want to live within your income. Stores are merchandised to entice you into buying without thinking. If you give in, you'll find yourself with lots of things you really don't need and didn't particularly want—and you'll have limited your cash flow.

Another way to ensure living within your income is to save a certain amount of each paycheck. Some companies have an automatic system for this, whereby you can earmark a percentage of each paycheck to go directly into savings without your ever seeing it. This works well, especially if you're in the transitional phase of getting control of your finances. What you don't see, you won't spend. Once you're on top of the financial situation, you can save any way you like, even shop around for the best interest rates in town. As a minimum, experts advise you to have at least six months' salary saved—and that's not taking into account any saving you might want to do for special major purchases or the annual vacation. That's money that should just sit in the bank, there for you in case of an emergency.

For a woman unused to managing money, making $35,000 a year can seem like an unlimited fortune, but in fact, it's a finite amount that can disappear down the rabbit hole if it's not managed properly.

We've talked about living up to your income, but there are many people who go beyond it, into bankruptcy. Spending against future earnings is a prerogative only the government has these days. For individuals, deficit spending is a disaster. Eventually financial excesses catch up with you.

On the positive end of things, being in control of your money can give you a feeling of control over your life. For example, Bettye always has a percentage of money put away so that if she wanted to quit her job tomorrow and take a vacation or a rest or take her time looking for something else, she could do it comfortably. Many of the women we spoke to had this kind of cushion. It's reassuring to know you can walk away if you want to.

People who live up to or beyond their incomes become slaves

to that income. They can't walk away from it, ever, because they can't afford to.

If money is properly managed, it becomes part of your support system, a line of defense against the variables in your life. If you lose your job or your husband does, you have financial options. If you want to buy a new house or refurbish your present one, you can do it. If your marriage ends in divorce, you can pick up the pieces and begin a new life, free of the stress of financial problems. No one likes to think about the bad things that can happen, but bad things happen to people every day and there should be some "rainy day" planning in your financial strategy.

Carol has had a career for more than thirty-five years. So has her husband, Roy. Together they have earned quite a lot of money. Two of their three children have finished college, and the third is about to enter. Last year Roy lost his job. He's been looking for a year for the right position—at his level and age, the right position doesn't come along every day. Because they had saved and invested their money wisely, Carol and Roy haven't had to worry about money. They've adjusted their budget and have been more careful with spending, but they haven't had to panic. "One thing that really helped is that in thirty-five years we never lived on my salary," Carol says. "We just banked it or invested it. We always had what we needed, but we didn't overspend. Since my salary could easily support a family of five, we had quite enough in the bank for Roy to take his time looking for another job."

Needless to say, although Roy may have felt some stress over being unemployed, he didn't have the added tension of wondering how he was going to support his family.

Controlling Your Money Means Planning

Those of us who are thirty-five or younger are part of the Me Generation, the postwar baby boom that is used to getting everything NOW. Our parents were part of the Depression generation, and they took much more easily to planning because they had experienced the hard times during the Depression. For those of us who are part of the baby boom, there was all feast, no famine. We're used to getting what we want. And that means it can be harder for us to plan.

Nevertheless, it's necessary, and once you get used to it, it's fun because financial planning is a strategy, just as getting ahead in your career or managing your family is a strategy. If you figure it all out right, you win.

Money is a means of getting what you want. Whatever it is that you want, you'll have to plan your money to get it. For a single woman with no dependents, this kind of planning is relatively simple. She decides what she wants and budgets for it. For a couple, it becomes more complex because there are two incomes and two sets of wants. This calls for joint decision making and sometimes some compromise. However, if you are compatible enough to be married, the compromises won't be all that distasteful, and your financial planning is still relatively simple, given two fairly disciplined adults.

When you have children, the planning becomes more complex. For starters, the initial decision to have a child needs a plan. If both parents are working, will the mother work through her pregnancy and after the birth of her child? Planning on one income or two will make a big difference. Having a baby costs money. Many companies have maternity benefits plans, with varying amounts taken care of. You need to know what is covered by your company's plan or by your husband's to know what the birth itself will cost you.

Beyond that, every detail, large and small, will cost money, from furniture for the baby's room to live-in or part-time help (or at least baby-sitters), to doctors' visits, etc. And that's just the short-term financial planning. For the long term, you will have to figure on an additional person to house, feed, clothe, educate, entertain, etc. Some parents set up trust funds or annuities that mature in time for their children's college educations. That kind of long-term planning makes sense.

Beyond the decision to have one child is the decision whether to have more. If more are planned, they must be figured into the financial scheme.

People who are really in control of their lives will want to be in control of when they have children and how many they have. And the family budget will be a major factor.

For the Me Generation, the choice to have a child or children may mean deferring some of the other things they want out of life—short-term or long-term. Of course, children bring their own many, varied rewards, but the expenses incurred for them should be seen as trade-offs for other things the couple might do with that money.

Who Controls the Money?

If you're single and unattached, the answer to that question is easy—you do! You may have an accountant, a lawyer, a banker, and an investment counselor to advise you, but you make the final decisions.

While we're on the subject of advice, we should point out that any expertise you can take advantage of is worth having. There are numerous books on financial planning, investments, etc., but some solid professionals from whom you can seek counsel are invaluable. No one person is an expert on everything. The management of money is a specialized field. You go to a doctor for any illness you may have, you seek a good auto mechanic to repair your car, a lawyer to handle legal matters, and in the same way, you can go to money professionals for advice and services. For example, a good accountant can show you how to pay your fair (and legal) share of taxes without paying any unnecessary amounts. He can take a look at your budget and give you pointers, can tell you whether you should incorporate yourself or not, can check the books of any business you're planning to buy. Once you find a good accountant, he can be a resource for life, from simple to more complex matters.

As there are more and more people with disposable incomes, a whole new industry is burgeoning: money managers. They will advise you on how to save or invest your money in anything from the stock market to real estate. Some will deal with fairly modest amounts; others will accept accounts of no less than a quarter of a million dollars. But if you have disposable income that you want to see grow, you might consult a money manager. Be sure to check his or her credentials and, if possible, to get a recommendation from someone you know and trust. And be sure you understand what he or she wants to do with your money. Don't just take him on faith. At worst, he could be dishonest. But he could also make a mistake. It's best to use even a financial manager as an adviser, not a guru.

More and more banks are offering money management courses and counseling services. These should at least be looked at as good sources of financial advice.

As a single career woman, with or without advice, you make the final decisions concerning your money. But what happens when you marry or live with someone? As we've seen from the Michele Marvin case, even living with someone can have legal and financial ramifications, and certainly, if you're married, your resources are joined. Given that framework, how do you manage the money?

With the women we interviewed who were married, some of them did the family finances, and some had their husbands do it, but in all cases these women knew where the money was going.

That's the key, and it's another application of dealing through strength, which we've talked about before. It's neither fair nor practical to make one partner bear the full burden of financial management. Although one of you may actually pay the bills, you both should know where the money is going.

In some two-income marriages, husband and wife may keep separate checking accounts and actually split expenses.

Judy and George do this. "I have my own checking and savings account," Judy says. "George has his own. We will soon have a joint savings account. He owns a house that I insisted my name not be on because I did not pay for it. He wants my name on it. I'm coming to terms with that. . . . We clearly control our own money. I control more of it on a maintenance level; he controls it more on a growth level. When he is installing new bathrooms, he's paying for all of that. I will pay ongoing food bills, utilities, all that sort of thing. He will pay for all the liquor.

"I said to him from the outset, 'Look, I'd just as soon buy the food. I don't want joint anything. If I run into problems, I will let you know. I expect you to pay for any new acquisitions.' I think it works out very well. We've never measured it."

Other couples have more joined financial dealings. Bettye and Charlie pool their resources. Because he is in banking, he handles the bill paying, but they make long-term financial plans together, consider new acquisitions and investments together.

Peter and Joyce do the same thing. Their finances are joined, but no major financial decisions are made unilaterally by either one.

For many people, the subject of money has almost more taboos than sex. They were taught not to talk about it as children, and consequently, as adults many people find it hard to be open about money, even in a marriage. Obviously this kind of openness is necessary, whether finances are separate or joined. You need to talk about money before you can do any financial planning. And since money is the means of supporting your life, if you're sharing your life together, money matters shouldn't be secrets you keep from each other.

Karen knew her second marriage was destined to fail when her husband refused to share money matters with her. He grudgingly gave her food money weekly, and that was it. She had no idea what he had in savings, even in income. In fact, for several years they filed separate tax returns. "It always seemed like a temporary relationship," says Karen. "And it eroded my trust fast. We lived in his house, which needed a lot of work to make it livable, but I decided not to put my money into his house. We stayed together for ten years, but the marriage was over the day I realized he really didn't want to share his life with me."

We've already talked about the importance of trust in a marriage. Sharing money matters is clearly an example of putting your money where your mouth is.

For Love or Money or Both?

How much does money really mean to you? Where does it rank in your top ten values? What would you do for money? What wouldn't you do?

We believe money is a means to an end. It's a necessary commodity, but it's only one of the means of having it all and certainly not an end in itself. But it's a highly personal question. We've heard for years about the men who "sell out" for money in business; in textbooks, novels, and movies we've been saturated by the greed-versus-integrity question. Now that women can have careers, what kinds of choices will they have to make about what's important to them, personally and professionally?

Situation: You've just been offered a job that pays $20,000 more than you now earn. You're in public relations, but the job you are being offered is in marketing. You really love public relations, and from what you know about marketing, you're not crazy about it. But there's the money to consider. What do you do?

Situation: You've just been offered your dream job—head of personnel for a major corporation at which you will get the chance to implement all those ideas that ABC Corporation just ignored. You are head of personnel there, and since it's a larger company, you are making substantially more money than this new dream job offers. What do you do?

Having it all involves having options, then making the choices that make you happy. Of course, there are financial realities. However, if you're living within your means, all things being equal, you shouldn't have the need to go after the big money, no matter what the job is, unless money is a higher value to you than job satisfaction.

The happiest people we've met are those who are getting paid what they're worth, doing work they really enjoy. In all the current studies done on work-related stress, the greatest cause of the stress was lack of job satisfaction. Remember, money is a means to an end. It won't in itself make you happy although it may give you the financial means to get whatever it is that would make you happy. But if you get caught in the big-money-at-any-cost trap, you may find that the emotional price you pay isn't worth the extra cash.

It's a rare and precious thing to be paid for doing work you'd want to be doing anyway. Joyce had that experience as a journalist. "Some days I just couldn't believe someone was paying me for doing this work, because I love it so much. Even when there were problems, I loved it. The satisfaction was tremendous. I don't ever remember being mentally tired. Physically tired, yes. But never mentally tired. The work sustained me and fed me."

Karen feels the same way about writing novels. "It's what I love to do. Of course, I want to make money doing it, and of course, sometimes the writing gets tough. But I love it."

Maria feels that way about preparing gourmet delights. "Ever since I was a child, I've been fascinated by fine cooking. I learned from my mother and grandmother and just kept building on what they had taught me. I get such enjoyment out of it even though it is a killing business, especially when you want everything to be perfect."

In the best of all possible worlds you make the most money doing the thing you love best. A major way women can feel in control of their careers is to learn how to negotiate the money they deserve for doing what they love. Asking for that raise or those executive perks is a skill that women can learn from men. They can also have an advantage by doing their homework in surveying the going market rate for their services. The better they are at what they do and the better they are at *merchandising* what they do, the more in demand they will be and the more their salaries will rise, if not in their present company, then with a smart competitor who knows a valuable employee when he or she sees one.

But if the choice ever really comes down to job satisfaction versus money, we think the people who go for job satisfaction come out the long-term winners. We've seen plenty of men and women get burned out quickly, working day after day at jobs that didn't suit them. The pressure and emotional stress can get pretty heavy—and as a rule of thumb, the more you're getting paid for a job, the more potential pressure and stress there is. If the job doesn't suit you, then you have to act like someone else to get things done— and that cuts you off from who you are. In the end, the person spending all that extra money may not be the person who started out to earn it.

The Company's Money Versus Yours

Between high-level deals and executive perks, you may find you have to shift gears financially at the end of the workday. At the office, you may have the power to spend a million or two of the company's money, but if you keep thinking in those terms, your next shopping expedition could be a disaster.

At the office, it may be perfectly okay to hire a limousine to take you to the airport or a business affair. However, if you start expecting that kind of perk in your personal life, you may find limousines eating up your discretionary income.

Even dining out on the company can be a trap if you can't shift gears from your professional to your personal life. We work for a company where all business lunches and dinners are done in a first-rate way. We frequent only the very best restaurants in New York, and, believe us, you get used to it. However, we also know how to separate that from a quiet dinner out with our husbands or, for Bettye, with the family. Since we both enjoy dining out on a regular basis, we know that every meal can't cost $80 or $100 for two.

Separating your means from the financial means of your company is important. Otherwise, you may constantly be trying to live beyond yourself to compete with the corporate you. And your perspective can become warped. When you're talking about millions of dollars in the office, a thousand-dollar personal expense seems like peanuts, but if it's coming out of your pocket, you'd better be able to afford it as if it were peanuts, or you're in big trouble.

Joyce once worked for a company the president and owner of which told his assembled staff that they all should try flying the Concorde immediately. Of course, from his vantage point, the few thousand dollars it would cost were merely spending money, but for the staff it represented a major investment. Needless to say, no one followed up on his advice.

Dealing with Money and Status

Many of us on the career path have discovered that money is power. And we're learning to enjoy it, but we also need to learn how to deal with it in a smart and ladylike way (in the same way men should be gentlemanly about it). The amount a woman earns is some measure of her success. She may feel justifiably proud of her financial accomplishments and may genuinely delight in spending her money. The trick is not to flaunt it and not to be indiscreet about it.

With women enjoying their newfound camaraderie and sisterhood, there is an impulse to share all, even with co-workers. Take our advice. Avoid sharing information about your salary with colleagues. Companies pay people both what they are worth and what they demand for their services. It is each person's responsibility to negotiate his or her salary, raises, etc. An employee would be justifiably outraged if her boss went around telling other workers what her salary was. In the same way, your boss would have every right to be angry at you for telling co-workers the salary you and he or she negotiated for you. It's just not a fair thing to do.

Aside from its not being fair, discussing your salary with co-workers can have disastrous consequences. For one thing, if your boss finds out, he or she will be angry at you, lose some measure of trust in you, and have serious doubts about your ability to be discreet—none of which will help you in terms of future advancement or raises. Secondly, don't expect your co-workers to be overjoyed if you are making more for doing the same work. Envy and hostility could result. And to what purpose? Some things are personal and confidential. Your salary fits into that category, especially where co-workers are concerned.

In terms of flaunting money, it's just tacky and tasteless and does nothing to endear you to anyone—from co-workers to family and friends. If you have money, enjoy it. But don't make a show of it or talk endlessly about how well you're doing or how much you can afford to buy.

A friend of ours who works for an accounting firm told us this story. A co-worker of hers had been taken to lunch by a new accountant in the office—a young woman from a fabulously wealthy family. This colleague was a divorced mother of two, struggling to keep the family finances afloat. The new accountant knew her situation. Nevertheless, after they had lunch, the accountant trotted her off to an exclusive jewelry store, where she purchased a necklace for $3,000, then casually asked the co-worker, in front of the salesperson, whether she wanted one put aside for herself as well. The co-worker felt she had been publicly humiliated and decided that the new accountant had just lost her friendishp. She deserved to. Anyone who is not on top of her money enough to avoid playing destructive power games with it deserves to be disliked. And you can bet the co-worker lost no time in telling the rest of the staff what had happened.

Many as a Symbol of Independence

To be truly independent, a woman must be able to pay her own way. In that sense, money is a newfound symbol of independence. It enables her to set her life course, to pursue and plan for various options, to have a sense of security about her present and her future. But merely *earning* money isn't enough to make her feel independent. Being in control of it is the only way her independence will be a fact, not just a symbol.

If you're not totally in control of your finances now, you should make it a top priority. There are a number of books, espeially designed for women, available on the market. Check your local library or bookstores for the best ones. Consult experts—your banker, your lawyer, your accountant. If you don't have any of these, thing seriously about getting one or all. Understand all your options with money before taking action.

Karen invested in the stock market at the suggestion of a relative who also recommended a stockbroker. Karen didn't know anything about the market, except that her instincts said she should stick with blue chip stocks. "But the broker said no," Karen told us. "He advised me to get into the options market. I was so naïve. I didn't realize that what he wanted was his commission every time I told him to buy or sell. In less than a year I lost twenty thousand dollars. I learned my lesson. I just wasn't ready for the stock market. I didn't know enough to make intelligent decisions."

Do your homework, and decide very carefully how you want your money to work for you. If you have a limited amount to invest and can't afford to lose it, stay away from risky, speculative investments. Sure, you may win big, but you may also lose big. If you can't afford to lose it, don't risk it.

Some women fear money because they never mastered mathematics. If you're one of them, face it and fix it. Take a business math course or an accounting or bookkeeping course. Think of all the skills you've acquired over the years. There's nothing you can't learn. If you don't feel comfortable with numbers and don't know how to work with them, you'll never feel comfortable with money.

Finally, plug into the women's network for some help and counseling. If you know of one or several women who seem to be on top of their finances, ask them how they do it—not how much they have or make, just the principles they use to manage their money.

The more comfortable you feel with money in your own life, the more professional doors will open for you. Traditionally women in business have not been in the financial areas (although that is changing now). But if you feel in control of your own budget, the departmental or divisional budget will just be more of the same on a larger scale.

Remember, you can't have it all if you don't know what it costs and what you can afford. Be in control of your means.

EIGHT

CHANGE
FOR BETTER
OR WORSE

I guess I'm less affected now by change than most people because my whole life has been a series of changes, unpredictable changes. I find myself always prepared for a battle. I've always had sort of an anxious feeling, I guess, waiting for the next change. But I've reached the point now where I don't go to bed without feeling at ease. I know I can cope with whatever new change comes along; I've coped with so many changes before.

I get nervous when I don't have change. I'm addicted to it. I've always traveled and moved. I usually just get up and change. I ask to be transferred, or I leave a job to go back to school or take another job. I've never been in any position longer than a year.

Maybe I am the ultimate rationalist, but I do feel change is positive. You grow from it. You redefine yourself. A lot of good things came out of my divorcing Tom. After Tom, I really knew that I didn't want to be living with or involved with men in their thirties. I felt they were crazy, groping their way the way everybody gropes. I didn't want to nurse another man through his career. Now I have greater perspective on it, but at the time I was devastated. Tom asked me for a divorce. I felt I had failed him somehow, failed as a woman somehow. At first I wanted him back, no matter what, even though he left me for another woman. Then, somehow, things began to change. I met a man, had an affair, felt like a woman again—an attractive woman—something I hadn't felt with Tom in a couple of years. After that first affair there were a couple of other men, and suddenly I realized Tom and I weren't right for each other. By the time he wanted to come back I just wanted out. My whole life changed, and although I didn't initiate the change, I certainly learned to cope with it and grow with it.

CHANGE, IN GREATER and greater frequency, is both the asset and the liability of the career woman. Our increased options give us more opportunities to effect change in our lives—in personal and professional areas. But the same options leave us open to changes from the outside—job relocation, getting fired, the breakup of a relationship, a new promotion.

Every living thing changes in some respect or another during the course of its life span. Sharpen your survival instincts. Start to view positive change as an opportunity to grow. Start to see negative change as an opportunity to develop and refine coping skills. Every living creature must make the basic choice: to grow or to stagnate. The desire for the status quo is really the desire for stagnation. Life is too precious to waste it standing still, while others are moving ahead, reaching out to grasp life's opportunities.

Change can be exhilarating or devastating. It is almost always stressful. And like stress itself, change can either strengthen you or wear you down. In the context of this book, we find that change and its crises are the true test of having it all. You take a step on your own, gather your support systems, deal through strength, and use all the skills and the knowledge at your disposal.

Change can be major or minor, self-initiated or other-initiated. When we talk about change, we'll be considering two major factors: the intensity of the change and the origin of the change. Aside from detailing the kinds of change there are and how people deal with them, the focus of the chapter is on how best to cope with it, prepare for it, keep your psyche in one piece, and survive it all.

The Princess and the Pea Syndrome

We all know the story of the little girl who was invited to spend the night in the castle. The queen tested her daintiness by placing a small pea under layers and layers of bedding. In the morning the girl proved that she was indeed a princess when she complained of her bad night's sleep.

How you deal with the little things in life can offer a major clue to your ability to cope with the big changes.

—Do you get upset if your secretary makes an appointment for you and the person appears unannounced?
—Do you go up the wall if your office is rearranged without your being notified?
—Do you have to hide your displeasure when your husband makes last-minute plans for you?
—If your boss asks you to prepare for a business meeting in two hours, are you thrown into a panic?

If your answer to most or all of the above is yes, watch out! You're going to have some real problems with major changes. On the other hand, if you think those questions were a breeze, it doesn't mean that you're immune. What follows is a systematic classification of change and its effect on career women.

Change Quotient Factor Identification Chart

1-1	minor change—you caused to happen
1-2	minor change—someone caused to happen to you
2-1	major change—you caused to happen
2-2	major change—someone caused to happen to you

There are four dimensions in change: Their intensity is measured as major or minor, and their origin comes from the self or from another. Let's take a look at the number codes in the chart:

1-1 Change: The first digit refers to the intensity or importance of the change. The first digit symbolizes minor change. The second digit signifies that the change was initiated by you. For example, you changed the time or place of a meeting.

1-2 Change: Again, the first digit symbolizes minor change. But the second digit signifies that someone else made the change. For example, your secretary scheduled an appointment for you but forgot to tell you about it.

2-1 Change: The first digit refers to the intensity of the change. In this case, the 2 signifies a major change. The second digit, 1, indicates the major change was initiated by you. For example, you decide to divorce your husband.

2-2 Change: The first digit refers to a major change. The second digit indicates the change was initiated by someone else. For example, your husband decides to divorce you.

In the area of major change, the 2-2 Change is the most difficult to deal with. Even though the 2-1 Change indicates major change, since you have initiated the change, you are in control, and the change is a means of getting what you want—you change jobs or relocate or decide to have a child. In the 2-2 Change, something major is changing in your life, but you haven't initiated it. You must react to it, but you're not in control of the change. For example, you're fired, or someone close to you dies, or your husband asks you for a divorce.

Yes, people get through these kinds of major changes, but how do they do it? What inner resources and strengths do they call upon? What makes one person cope better with change than others? It may help to identify your attitudes toward change in a larger perspective. We've identified three major types. Most of us fall into some combination of these.

The Changeling: The changeling deals with 1-1 Change without a problem; she even likes it. After all, change is the spice of life, and she likes to play a bit. If things stay the same too long, she'll get bored and try to initiate change to stir up a little excitement. She deals with 1-2 Changes with little difficulty. In fact, if the minor change makes things better or more interesting, she's sorry she didn't think of it herself. If she's feeling daring, she may even initiate a few 2-1 Changes. She may change her job, move to another city, give up one man for another. She lives life at a fast pace and expects others to keep up. If they can't, that's their problem. 2-2 Changes throw her, maybe not as much as they would throw everyone else, but they upset her for several reasons:

—Someone else has done something *to* her; she was not the initiator of the change.

—It may upset her planning and interrupt or affect other parts of her life.

—If it's a negative 2-2 Change, she'll feel pain, be hurt.

What helps her cope is her long experience and the practice with change that she has initiated herself. She feels at home with the phenomenon of change, so even if the major change is negative, she's on more familiar ground, psychologically, than someone who avoids change.

The Changeable: The Changeable feels a little flurry in her stomach when she must make a 1-1 Change. She likes things to run smoothly, and her idea of "running smoothly" is that things stay the same. However, when it's necessary, she'll initiate a 1-1 Change, and she deals with it well, even though deep down she doesn't like it. A 1-2 Change distresses her a little. While she wouldn't fly into a rage if a meeting time or place were changed, she wouldn't like it, and she'd probably demand an explanation. For example, if the president of the company asked her to attend a meeting and he changed the meeting place, she would cope quietly. If she had organized the meeting and her secretary had to change the meeting place and forgot to tell her, she would be more vocal in her objections. As boss or employee she adheres to the theory of No Surprises, stating simply, "I won't surprise you, and don't you surprise me. I like to know what to expect."

She would think long and hard before precipitating a 2-1 Change, although in the long run she would probably make it. She might ask friends for advice or seek professional help before making any final decisions. She takes change seriously. She'll cope with it if she has to, but she doesn't go looking for it.

Because of her inner strength, she would get through a 2-2 Change after a period of adjustment, but that period would be difficult, and she'd probably seek friendly help or professional guidance. Even a major positive change initiated by someone else would have a disquieting effect since she likes things to stay the way they are. If her boss approached her with a relocation/promotion proposal, she would probably accept if it bettered her career considerably, but the adjustment would be tough, and in the long run she might be unhappy because so much of her life is built around things staying the same.

The Unchanging: The Unchanging almost never initiates even the most minor changes. She probably gives more thought to making very exact arrangements because she's learned that making any kind of change is simply not worth it to her. Once a meeting is scheduled, in her mind it is *scheduled*, and nothing short of a disaster should change it. If she is successful, it's because she's already figured out, even if only subconsciously, that she has an awful reaction to change, and she makes every effort to avoid it. She has to initiate and cope with minor changes when necessary and works on handling these minor kinds of change because she knows she must demonstrate a certain degree of flexibility if she is to be successful.

She is bothered by 1-2 Changes. To protect herself, she has chosen to deal with very reliable people whenever possible. She has landed a job in a structured environment and fights to keep it that way. She flies into a rage (although she may not show it) if she finds that her secretary has rearranged an appointment. She becomes equally upset if a peer decides to change a meeting place or time. She manages to cope when her boss does the changing, but it bothers her—and in all probability she is ulcer-prone because the flexibility necessary to get through life is missing from her makeup.

She would almost never initiate a 2-1 Change. She would have to be grossly dissatisfied with the status quo to do so, and even then she would do it only after substantial internal agonizing and probably professional help.

A 2-2 Change would be devastating. Coping would be possible but very difficult for her, and it would take her a substantial amount of time to adjust to the change. Her stress level during a 2-2 Change would be much higher than that of the Changeling or the Changeable. She'd have to nurture herself and rely heavily on the nurturing provided by already established support systems.

Making the First Move

Most people will fit into one of the three categories we've described. If you're most like the Changeling, then, while you can certainly learn some new pointers on coping with change, it's not a subject that threatens you. If you identify with the Changeable or Unchanging, don't give up or despair. While you may never become a Changeling, you can learn to cope more effectively with change by identifying the fears or problems you have with it. You can also practice feeling comfortable with change by initiating some 1-1 Changes to strengthen your flexibility. Since change is sure to occur, it's best to deal with it in the most positive way you can.

If you're afraid of change, admit it; then cope with it. When Joyce made the decision to move to Ohio, she was scared. It was new territory for her, and she knew she'd have to make it on her own. Admitting the fear helped her cope with it. She refused to let it paralyze her, and she came away from the experience knowing that she had tested herself to new limits—and she'd passed the test. She also plugged into friends and family for the support she needed. One of our principles for coping with change: Plug into Whatever or Whomever—the important thing is to feel secure. The bigger the change, the greater the need for the security of the known.

Plugging into Support Systems

Even Wonder Woman doesn't face the world unarmed and alone. She has her magic bracelets and her magic lariat and her mothers and sisters on that far-off magical island. You don't have to face the world alone either. When major change occurs, positive or negative, don't try to tough it out alone. Even a great new job or promotion brings with it feelings of anxiety. Share the joy, but share the negatives as well.

When we were writing this book, we were both excited and anxious. Excited, because it was something new for us, a chance to communicate ideas we believed in and wanted to share with other women. But we were also scared. Could we do it? Would it be good? As collaborators we formed our own support system with each other. We also relied on our husbands.

When big changes occur in your life, whether you initiate them or someone initiates them for you, plug into friends, family, loved ones. Seek professional help if you need to. Talk to a minister if it will help you. Even go back to a place you know and love to gather your inner resources. Most important, try to talk to someone who's experienced the same kind of change.

When Joyce began her job in Ohio, the first few days were tough on her emotionally. A phone call from her cousin cheered her considerably. "My stomach always cramps for the first few days on a new job," he said. He'd described her symptoms exactly, and obviously he'd survived and succeeded. Because he shared his experience with her, she felt she wasn't alone, that what she was feeling was okay.

As important as that support is during a positive change in your life, it is one hundred times more important during a negative change, especially one you didn't initiate.

Cindy went through a dreadful experience. She had been divorced several years before and was living with her two small boys when she met Gil. She couldn't get over him. They liked all the same things in the same way, he loved her, he loved her children; she had been struggling to make ends meet, and he was wealthy enough to take care of her and the boys. Most of all, she loved him. She could talk about nothing and no one else. They set the wedding day, sent out the invitations, planned the honeymoon, and then everything ended. Gil was killed in a car accident while visiting his family.

Cindy had always been a person who could cope with just about everything. But this paralyzed her. And none of us knew what to say. She kept crying, saying she wished that her life were over, that she couldn't go on; she just didn't know what to do next.

Desperately we tried to figure out a way to help. What we finally thought of was another friend who had lost her husband. She had had the same feelings, but she'd managed to survive and come out the other end. She agreed to call Cindy, and they talked for several hours. That didn't immediately heal all of Cindy's wounds. That would take a long time. But just knowing that someone else had survived what she was going through was a beginning.

Often, when you are going through a major change such as the death of a close family member, you can find groups of people who can share your experience with you. Certainly the first step into one of their meetings, or even getting on the phone, can be painful. But in the long run it will be worth it. You can find someone to talk to, who will support you, whom you can support.

Change—for better or worse—can be traumatic, a shock to the system. Part of having it all is bringing balance into your life, and in times of change, the support of people you know and love can help you keep that balance until your psyche has adjusted to the major change.

The Major Career Changes

There are several kinds of major professional changes for the better. Some you initiate; some you don't. You can seek or accept a new job with another company or move to another city where opportunities are better. You can ask for a promotion within your company. With any of these changes, even though you initiate them, a lot of careful thought and planning should go into making the changes as smooth as possible.

Before accepting a better job at another company, find out all you can about it: what its style is, how well it is doing financially, how it treats its employees. What are the future opportunities there? Is there room for you to grow, or will you have to leave that company for your next promotion? Where do you want to be in five years? Does this new job bring you closer to your five-year goal? Is the salary better? What about the benefits? How much, if any, business travel is involved? How much would you like? How are women viewed by top management? Could you continue your career there if you became pregnant? Or if you have children, how does the company view career mothers? Will being a mother affect your future at the company? Certainly this isn't an exhaustive list of the questions you should be asking, but it indicates the range of your investigation.

Once you have the answers to all your questions and are satisfied that your prospective new company passes the test with flying colors, you should still give your current company an opportunity to make a counteroffer. There may be career opportunities you don't know about.

Once you've decided to leave, prepare yourself for feeling disoriented for the first couple of weeks on a new job. You won't know anyone, and you won't know where anything is. You'll also be the center of attention for the first week or so—as the new kid on the block. Try to give yourself a week or two between your present job and your new one, to catch your breath and gather your forces for your new position. Leaving one job on Friday and reporting for a new one on Monday gives you no chance to ease into change.

If you decide to relocate to a new city, find out as much about it as you can before making your decision. Visit several times. Talk to people who have lived and worked there. Have interviews lined up in advance if it's not possible to have a specific job offer before you go. Try to select a city where you know people. Or get names of people from friends, relatives, and business acquaintances. If you will really miss your friends and family, either choose a city fairly close to home, or adjust your budget to accommodate several visits and higher-than-normal telephone bills. Make sure your new city has a cost of living on a par with or lower than the city you're in. If that's not the case, make sure salaries are commensurately higher. Collect any written information you can: Chamber of Commerce pamphlets; real estate bulletins; several copies of the local newspaper. If you prefer one climate over another, make sure the city you choose has the climate that suits you. Remember the I Am Not My Job Principle, and don't choose a city only because career opportunities are better. How will you like the *rest* of your life?

If you get a promotion within your company, although a lot will be known, there will still be some change, even if it's mostly in the way your co-workers perceive you. Of course, your responsibilities will increase. You may have more people to manage, a wider territory to cover, a bigger budget. Try to find out as much as you can about what the promotion entails before accepting it. If you can, speak to the person who is currently in the job. Is he or she moving up, out, or on to another position? Whichever it is, try to find out why. What is your next step *after* this promotion?

The more you can anticipate the effects of a change, the more positive an experience it will be.

There are also major professional changes for the better that you don't initiate. For example, your company asks you to relocate or offers you a promotion. The same principles apply as when you ask for a relocation or promotion, except that you also have to deal with change initiated by someone else. Don't say yes immediately. Give yourself at least overnight to think about it. Consult with anyone you need to whose advice you value. Make sure that the move advances your career; otherwise, it may not be worth it to you.

When You Get Fired

In your professional life, probably no change can be more negative or traumatic, at least in the short term, than getting fired. Sometimes you can sense it coming, but you hope for the best. Other times it just happens, catching you totally unaware and unprepared. Your feelings are in a turmoil. Your pride is hurt; your ego is aching; you may feel anger at the injustice of it all or shock at the suddenness. Whatever you feel, the best course is to find out, as clearly and specifically as possible, why you've been fired. Listen to what's said; then evaluate for yourself whether or not you deserved to be fired. If you didn't, then what's happened is unfair and unfortunate, but you'll go on to bigger and better things. If you did deserve it, try to learn from the critique of your performance what you did wrong. Learning from mistakes can be helpful in the future. As angry as you may feel at the time, try not to burn any bridges behind you. Try to keep the firing as cordial as possible. You may need your present firm as a reference, or you may find yourself dealing with it in your next position. If you feel that your firing has been illegal in any way, put your reasons in writing to the personnel department.

Make sure of your facts and of the law. Seek legal counsel, if necessary, to see what your next course of action should be. If there's no legal action to be taken, as quickly as you can, start exploring what's next. If you're plugged into your network of business associates, they'll be able to tell you what's available and may even be able to help you with a lead or two. If your résumé isn't current (and it always should be), get it up to date and professionally typed and printed. Focus as much as you can on the positive aspects of the future. Gain control of the situation as quickly as you can. For one thing, it will stop you from feeling like a victim or a failure. For another, it will transform negative energy into positive energy by forcing you to get on with your life. Talk to friends and family for support, but don't whine. Take the time to write down all your career options at this point and the routes you can take to get to them. Remember that many others have been fired before you and they survived.

Preparing Yourself and Others for Change

Most of us prefer the management system called No Surprises. We've mentioned it before. The definition is inherent in the title: "For whatever is coming, bad or good, give me some notice." You can apply this principle to your personal life as well.

Generally a 2-2 Change isn't something that happens over-night. For example, if something is really wrong with your marriage, you know it. You try all the possible solutions: talking to your husband; seeking professional help or counseling; talking to friends. At some point you make the decision that it just isn't going to work. At that point you should start preparing family, friends, and yourself for the change that's about to occur. Do as much as you can to make it as easy as possible on yourself and those you care about, knowing that even with preparation, it's going to be difficult. Even the Changeling, who loves change, is thrown by a 2-2 Change, so don't make it any harder on yourself and those you care about than you have to.

Use the same approach when you initiate a major change to prepare those who will be affected by the change. When Mona and her husband, Frank, knew they would be relocating to another city, their major concern was how to break it to their son, Michael, who finds change very difficult to deal with (an Unchanging if we ever met one). This is how Mona and Frank handled it:

"Michael was eight when we relocated to New York from Chicago. Knowing how difficult it is for him to cope with even minor changes, I planned everything down to the smallest details.

I didn't even mention the relocation until we had found a house, selected a school for Michael, found the church we would attend, and checked out the neighborhood for children his age that he could play with.

"When we finally explained what we were doing, we took Michael to New York to see how everything was set up. Although he still had an adjustment period, it was eased considerably by our showing him how we had solved most of the problems in advance."

Whether you'd take Mona and Frank's approach or not, the point is they thought about their son's feelings before thrusting him into change. They were sensitive to his needs and did everything they could to make the change as positive an experience as it could be.

The Seven-, Six-, Five-, ... One-Year Itch

As you've seen from our chart, some people could do without change and never miss it. But others need it, even thrive on it. If you're one of those, how do you know when you need a change? And what do you change? For starters, you apply one of our basic principles. You look inside yourself to see what you want. You look outside yourself to see whether the change you want is possible and makes sense. If the inside and the outside don't gel, you take another look.

Everyone's need and capacity for change are different. But it's important to know when you need change in your life, what you need, how to effect it in the best way possible. You also need to know when you need stability in your life or the absence of major change. This is an especially crucial point to remember if major changes are occurring simultaneously in several areas of your life. If you can, try to delay some of the changes, and take them one at a time. If you can't, realize at the outset that you're under multiple stress and you'll need to think and act a bit more slowly, to let yourself digest all of what's happening to you or even what you're causing to happen. Indulge yourself with as many positives as you can. Monitor your needs. For some people, multiple major change means they need more sleep or more alone time. For others, it means they need to be surrounded by those they love. For still others, it means getting away from the action, for a day or a weekend, or a week, to sort things out, catch their second emotional wind before getting back into the midst of change.

The worst thing to do when a major change occurs is to mask your symptoms of stress. We all know the escape routes—pills, liquor, compulsive work, compulsive partying, a toughing-it-out façade that doesn't let anything in or out. You need to let yourself feel whatever it is you're feeling without judging yourself by some mythical standard. If you need to cry, cry. If you need to talk, talk. If you need to be alone, ensure the time alone. It's always important to be tuned into yourself, but it's critical during times of major change—for better or worse.

In the Arms of the Old Girls' Network

We've talked about the need for support systems and advocated forming or plugging into the Old Girls' Network of fellow career women, but in this chapter we want to stress how necessary and important a network and support system are for coping with change.

Whether you are a Changeling, a Changeable, or an Unchanging, in times of major change you need people to talk to, people who have been through whatever is happening to you and can help you cope with it. Use your support systems and your Old Girls' Network to nurture you in times of stressful change. After all, that's what helping one another is all about.

For example, Bettye plugged into women who had worked while they were pregnant when she was pregnant with Ashley. She realized it would help to talk to people who had been through pregnancies and had maintained careers. She called women who had been referred to her by other women because she didn't know anyone who had done what she was doing. "It worked," she says. "Most people are flattered when you call and say, 'I am a friend of Sally's, and she recommended I call you and talk about something we have in common. I would like your advice. How did you handle the situation I'm in?' In short, you ask for help. Most women will respond to that kind of plea."

Bettye says that she has formed close friendships with some of the women who helped her at the period of major change in her life.

Pat uses the women's network whenever "something is gnawing at me and I can't quite identify what it is, whenever I am undergoing any kind of major change, whenever I feel I'm over my head. Basically my support system is made up of several levels: people who are a whole bunch smarter than I am in business. I need them because I tread on unbroken territory a lot, and I seek their advice: women at my own age and career level that I have a give-and-take relationship with. We act as sounding boards for each other. I filter and synthesize their advice, rather than take it as gospel, since we have the same experience level, and I also plug into women who are on a more junior level than I am. This may sound strange, but I believe I can learn a lot from them, and in turn, I'm able to pass on to them some of what I've learned from experience. I really believe that I should pay my dues, or somehow my luck might get shut off. It works for me."

Change Means Saying Hello and Good-Bye

Often major change can mean ending one phase of your life and going on to another. Mothers can identify with this. As their children leave home, their role as mother recedes, leaving them time to enjoy possibly the role of wife or career woman or both. On the other hand, they miss their children and their heightened role of motherhood.

The same kind of change happens to all of us. We all start out as workers. Then, suddenly, one day we get our first supervisory position and then our first management position. We can find that a mentor has become a peer. Sometimes our friends change. Or one marriage ends and another begins. Or we trade a single lifestyle for the commitment of marriage. Or we change a marriage of two into a family of three by deciding to have a child. Whatever the new things change brings to us, constructive, healthy change also means being able to let go. To trade off some pleasures of the past for pleasures of the future. To allow our priorities and loyalties, our feelings and commitments to shift as our lives change, as we grow and learn more.

It's all healthy and normal and part of life and to be expected, but that letting go can be wrenching if you haven't realized it's a part of change.

Just remember that having it all means letting go of some things, while grasping others. The trick is to sort out the constants from the variables and keep what's necessary and important to your life.

NINE

THE CAREER WOMAN'S BLUES

"You've come a long way, baby," the cigarette ad tells us. And in a lot of ways it's true. We're out there, in the real world, meeting daily challenges, having success after success, living the perfect life, where everything we've learned, every shred of advice we've been able to gather, has been faithfully applied so that we do everything right. We're the Golden Girls they used to make those 1940s movies about. Not only are we the president of the company, but every hair is in place, and our kitchens are clean. Ask any career woman. She'll tell you.

Oh, boy, will she!

If you think this book—or any book, for that matter—is going to make you perfect or make life ideal, forget it. We're here to tell you that having it all has its ups and downs, just like everything else in life. If you were expecting Superwoman, sorry, but she's busy on another planet, one where there are no husbands, no children, no time-consuming jobs, no sinks that back up—in short, no problems. Of course, she is also bored out of her mind.

We, on the other hand, are never bored. We are sometimes tired, sometimes harried, sometimes defeated, sometimes triumphant, sometimes chic, and sometimes messy, but we are never, ever bored. We don't have time to be bored. There are enough of life's little ironies to keep us laughing, crying, and coping for the rest of our days. Luckily we manage to laugh more than we cry, cope more than we don't. But if you ever feel that maybe all this juggling belongs in the circus, not in your living room, then you'll know what we mean when we mention the Career Woman's Blues. Any career woman who says she's never experienced them is either lying or in a coma. You say you still don't know what we're talking about? Let us give you a few examples. We'll start with ourselves.

There was the time Joyce had a very important job interview with a senior vice-president. She dressed carefully in her tailored suit and shirt in the prescribed neutral, nonoffensive color; her shoes were shined; every hair was in place; her makeup had been painstakingly applied (too much is cheap; too little is disaster in the fluorescent lights of most business offices). She carried all the necessary papers and credentials in her hand-tooled briefcase.

She set out a half hour early, to give herself plenty of time to make the train into New York. What she hadn't counted on was the world's biggest traffic jam. She sat helplessly in traffic as the minutes ticked away, her mind doing a mental countdown to the train's arrival time. Finally, she got off onto a side road, took a shortcut, and sped into the train station—in time to see the train pulling out. Quickly she considered her options. She could never beat the train to its next stop. If she drove straight into the city, she would still never make the appointment. It was hot. Her hair was beginning to droop, and her tailored suit was beginning to wilt.

She placed a call to the senior vice-president. She explained what had happened and how awful she felt. She said she'd make the next train, in an hour. He said he'd have only a few minutes to see her. She said that was all right. An hour and a half later they met in his office. There wasn't even time for her to sit down; he was late for a lunch date. Her carefully worked-out plan for making a good impression was going down the tubes, fast. He suggested they meet the next day. Luckily she got the job anyway, and the happy ending was made happier when her new boss told her that because she came into New York, knowing that she could see him for only a few minutes and was willing to return the next day, she got the job. Her perseverance had impressed him. The point is she got the job in spite of, not because of, her best-laid plans.

Bettye relates a different kind of experience. She was on her way into a policy meeting when she got a phone call from Ashley's school. Another child had hit her, and she was hurt. Could Bettye come to the hospital? She dashed into her boss's office, told him she had to run, and grabbed a cab to the hospital. Luckily all Ashley had suffered were a couple of scrapes and bruises. Bettye was able to take her home, leave her with her nanny, and run back to the office—in time for the meeting to be adjourned. Luckily she had an understanding boss, but Bettye says that was not exactly her day for feeling like Wonder Woman.

If you haven't figured it out yet, the Career Woman's Blues really refer to the times when you don't cope too well—or at least not according to plan. One thing you learn when you juggle lots of elements at once is that any of them can get beyond you at any given point in time. In Chapter One we talked about the importance of a sense of humor and perspective. The ability to laugh at ourselves and somehow muddle through, even when the situation seems impossible, is what really keeps us going on our pioneer trail.

We asked all the women we interviewed to share with us some funny or zany stories of times when the coping mechanism was tested to the fullest—and was sometimes found wanting.

Rebecca learned an important lesson about being a mentor. She's very funny as she tells the story now, but it wasn't funny at all at the time.

"When I worked at a major magazine, which shall remain nameless to protect my sanity, I met a young man, a fellow writer who I thought was very good but needed some polish to his writing style. He was very sympathetic to me in my problems adjusting to the rigid structure of this magazine, and I felt it was a sort of trading of support to help him with his writing. I even introduced him to a newspaper editor friend of mine, so that he would have a valuable contact for his free-lance writing efforts. She liked him and his work, and he ended up writing a weekly column for the newspaper. At the time he thanked me profusely for my efforts and said that he would be eternally grateful.

"Eternity apparently had a short run that season. I left the magazine a few months later to free-lance full time, and he got a job offer, largely as a result of his newspaper column, to be a major editor of a new magazine. He was in the position to buy a lot of free-lance articles, and when he first told me about his new job, he promised that I would be a primary source of that free lance.

"Weeks went by, and I didn't hear from him. When I called him, he said, 'Oh, sure, don't worry, I'll have lots of assignments for you.' And that's the last thing I ever heard. Luckily for me I had other outlets, but I felt he'd really let me down by not returning the favor after I had helped him. The more I thought about it, the more I realized that there were clues all along that he was a little too shallow and a little too glib to be a true business friend. I should have picked up on the signals and saved my help for someone who would have reciprocated."

The mother guilts can be a frequent source of problems for

career women. No matter how well adjusted they say they are to working while the kids are growing up, in a corner of their minds remains that nagging fear that maybe something will happen *because* they aren't home to supervise their children's every move.

Stephanie, a working mother with teenaged children, remembers the awful night she came home from work to find a policeman standing at her door. "Your son has been arrested for selling drugs," he told her.

"I thought to myself, 'Oh, no, how could this happen?' I hadn't even thought my son used drugs himself, and here was this policeman telling me that he was selling them. The mother guilts took over. I could hear my mother's voice saying, 'It's not right to work while your kids are growing up. They need you. You'll see, something terrible will happen if you're not there to watch them.' Was this divine—or mother's—retribution?

"I followed the policeman to the local police station and talked with my son. He denied the charge. It turned out later, after the police did a little investigating, that another boy, who really was selling drugs, had implicated my son to get himself off the hook. Luckily for us the truth was discovered, and my son was cleared, but I really put myself through hell, blaming myself for somehow failing my son by working.

"That incident happened a couple of years ago, and I think if something like that were to happen now, I wouldn't be so quick to blame it on the fact that I work. But you never know. The mother guilts are deep-seated and insidious. You can know in your head that it's okay to work, but somewhere in the pit of your stomach you still feel maybe there's something wrong with it."

Sometimes the juggling act can get so frenzied you almost don't know where you are or what you're supposed to be doing.

Bettye tells the story of the time she lived in Mexico and had to go on a business trip to Central America the week before Ashley's first birthday. She was determined to be home in time for her birthday party, but she hadn't counted on the somewhat sporadic scheduling of flights in the Latin American country she was visiting. When the time came to return home, her flight was canceled. There were no more flights until the next day. If she waited for the next flight, she would miss Ashley's party.

"I suppose it was a case of mother's guilt," she says. "I don't think Ashley would have been as disappointed as I would have if I'd missed the party. After all, she was only one and really didn't grasp yet the significance of a birthday. But I had promised her I'd be there, and I wanted to keep my promise.

"The airlines offered no help. They kept saying, 'Mañana.' Finally, I rented a jeep and a driver, drove across one country into another, and got a flight out of there to Mexico. It cost me a fortune, and the ride was a little hair-raising, but I fulfilled my supermom fantasy."

Most working mothers, especially those in the suburbs where they are in the minority, face the worry that their children will want to know why "their mommy is different."

Adele is a free-lance writer who works at home, and the mother of two boys. Her younger child came home one day with his latest school assignment. "Everybody drew pictures of their mommies today," he told Adele. "Here's my picture of you." It was all there in crayola—Adele as half woman, half typewriter.

When Joyce got married recently, the juggling act was two-sided. She was to go directly from a business meeting on a remote island off Florida to California to get married. Peter was to fly to California from New York on the same day, and they would meet at Los Angeles Airport. Why were two New Yorkers getting married in California? That's another story, and this one is complicated enough as it is.

"We were supposed to meet in California on a Saturday. The Tuesday before we were to meet, a major New York newspaper went on strike. Since Peter worked for its competitor, the strike, if it lasted, would mean that he couldn't get away. We put our plans on a wait-and-see basis even though my parents had already flown out to California to be there for the wedding. My cousin, who lives out there, had everything arranged, from the blood tests to the reception. I alerted everyone and hoped for the best.

"The next day I dashed out during a break in a meeting to call Peter to check the status of the strike. It was still on. And—more bad news—the government had just grounded all DC-Tens. He'd have to check his reservation to see whether or not he was on a DC-Ten. We connected at midnight that night, and there were two pieces of good news. The strike had been settled, and he was on a Seven-forty-seven.

"I alerted everyone in California. The wedding was on. The next morning, Thursday, I discovered that I couldn't make my scheduled flight out of Florida since there was no way to get to Tampa from the island I was on. All connecting flights to Tampa were booked. My company would have to make new reservations for me and would do its best to get me to California on Saturday.

"By Friday morning they told me the best they could do was a flight that got me into California on Saturday night. Not good enough. There were big plans for Saturday night, and I was determined to be there. I had them check again. They found there was a way to get me out if I were willing to leave the island at five fifteen A.M., take a short flight to Orlando, and connect with a flight to California that stopped in New Orleans. I would arrive in LA at ten-thirty A.M., Pacific time. Since Peter was arriving at two thirty in the afternoon, that would mean a four-hour wait at the airport. I checked with my cousin. He was willing to pick me up, give me a tour of LA, and return to the airport for Peter.

"In order to make the five-fifteen A.M. taxi, I had to get up at four thirty Saturday morning, the morning after a full week of nonstop meetings and a big final-night party. I packed between the last meeting session and dinner, went on to the party, and managed to fall into bed at about midnight.

"Somehow I got up at four thirty and traveled with three other unfortunates who couldn't escape the island any other way. I made the short flight to Orlando and managed to get on my connecting flight. By the time I arrived in California, although it was only midmorning their time, I had already been up and traveling for nine hours.

"All I wanted to do was collapse. However, I was met at the

airport by my cousin, my father, and my brother, all of whom were rarin' to go. We piled into my cousin's car and toured LA and Bel Air. Don't ask me what I saw. It was all a blur of lush, green Munchkin land.

"Finally, it was time to pick up Peter at the airport. At that point I had already put in a thirteen-hour day, but was it over? Of course not. From the airport we made the hour and a half drive to Newport Beach, where my cousin's wife and children were waiting to take us on a Fiberglass boat tour of Newport harbor. The tour took a couple of hours. Don't ask me what I saw—lots of boats and water and houses jammed close together. My apologies to Newport Beach, but my mind was barely functioning.

"From Newport Beach we drove to my cousin's home in Santa Ana to have dinner, then headed for the Orange County Airport to rent a car. By this time not only were my eyes closed but my teeth were clenched. It was midnight my time, and I'd been going for twenty and a half hours. My sense of humor had deserted me somewhere between LA Airport and Orange County Airport. But it wasn't over yet because Peter and I were staying at Laguna Beach, a half hour's drive from Santa Ana, and we didn't leave my cousin's house until midnight Pacific time—three A.M. my time.

" 'Oh, well,' I told myself in my best Scarlett O'Hara voice, 'tomorrow is another day. I'll just sleep in.' But that was before I learned about the horse show that my cousin's children were going to be in the next day. Of course, we would attend. And of course, we did. At eight the next morning we were on our way to sit in the scorching heat, but since too much of the same thing becomes boring, I'll spare you the details. The good news is we did get married as planned the following Tuesday, and luckily I had rested enough by then to enjoy it."

If we couldn't laugh at ourselves a little, we wouldn't have survived. Humor is a terrific safety valve, and any woman who can't take her lumps with good cheer will end up at Happy Valley or your local equivalent.

Take the story of Marcy, who, while on a five-country business trip, broke her leg. Since she was a computer sales representative and had to make her calls, this was no joke, but Marcy was able to treat it lightly. When her boss heard of her accident—she had tripped on the quaint cobbled steps of the quaint *pensione* she was staying at in Italy—he cabled her to come home. "No way," she cabled back. She continued her trip, using a wheelchair at first— "It made for first-class treatment at airports and just about everywhere I went," she told us—then switched to crutches and later to a walking stick. She not only finished her business trip but went on to vacation in North Africa and gave barely a thought to her leg.

Traveling abroad can provide lots of adventures, and as more and more women become involved in international business, they're taking more and more trips to countries all over the world. But these are not for the fainthearted.

Karen, an experienced traveler, went to Europe to do research on the novel she's currently working on. She had carefully planned her trip and booked it through a reputable travel agency she had used many times before. On this trip she was traveling with one of her daughters and her cousin. It seemed as if everything went wrong. They arrived at the Calais coach to find that even though they had reservations, the train company had no record of them. Good-bye, first-class compartment. Hello, tourist class, with its crowded, cramped quarters. And things got worse.

"When we arrived at the Channel crossing, it turned out only the first-class coach was going on the ferry. We had to get off the train, which at that point was at the end of a long pier. We walked about a mile, carrying all our luggage in the cold, damp drizzle of spring in England, and waited at the train station until we could make the crossing the next morning. After we crossed the Channel, we took another train to Paris. Since our plans had been really messed up, we didn't have a reservation, and again we were in second class. We were supposed to be met by a driver in Paris, but that was according to our old schedule. As it turned out, there was no one waiting for us, and since it was rush hour, we had to wait a long time to get a cab to our hotel. We all laugh about it now, but I was so furious at the time that I was ready to write a protest letter to the London *Times*, complaining about the treatment of tourists in England. I'm glad I didn't write the letter because I've always loved England, and of course, things can happen anywhere you go."

Occasionally tough times seem to go on and on. Take Susan's experience. She was working for a major retailer in a not-very-structured training program.

"After six months of basically folding merchandise in New York, I went to personnel and asked for some more meaningful training. After all, they had recruited me because I was a Harvard MBA, and they had me folding shirts and making change, with no end in sight. Nobody told me anything except 'Be patient,' and that's never been my strong suit.

"So I badgered personnel, and finally, after a couple of months, they told me I was going to Milwaukee as assistant without portfolio to a regional vice-president. I closed up my apartment in New York, rented an apartment in Milwaukee, shipped all my things there, and settled in. I knew no one and found it hard to meet people. My duties were unspecified and unclear, and no one, including myself, knew what to make of me or my position. After six months there, they asked me if I'd go to Pittsburgh on a temporary basis as acting manager of their store there since the manager had left. I kept my apartment in Milwaukee, because I had no idea how long I'd be in Pittsburgh, and rented a furnished room in Pittsburgh. Temporary turned out to be eight months. I had a work friend in Milwaukee who checked my apartment for me, to make sure it and all my worldly possessions were still there. I liked being acting manager, but I knew the position was temporary, and I was impatient to get back to Milwaukee, where home was for the moment.

"I should have known that that was too reasonable to happen. After eight months of living in a furnished room in Pittsburgh, I was transferred back to New York. I returned to New York by way of Milwaukee to close up my apartment and ship everything east again. I rented another apartment in New York—I had been gone just long enough for rents to go up about fifty percent, so that the apartment I got wasn't nearly as nice as the apartment I'd left a year before. Since I had lived and worked in three states during one year, I had to file tax returns in all three states.

"I was back in New York, but there still was no game plan for me. The man who had hired me had left, and no one seemed to care about my future. I was in merchandising—something I tried to avoid because I hated it. I stuck it out for another few months and finally left to go to Boston to work as a consultant."

For all the funny and not-so-funny horror stories that all of us can tell, we didn't find one woman who would want to change her life, past or present, in any fundamental way. It must be true that pioneers come from sturdy stock. Career women seem to thrive on adversity—or at least on overcoming and surviving it. We laugh as we swap stories about the way we were and are.

In a sense, our ability to laugh at ourselves is a sign of our coming of age. When women first began to have careers, their uncertainty and fear made it impossible to laugh at themselves. Every hurt or slight or setback seemed fatal. Now we've had a chance to be tempered by life, to experience success and failure, and we've learned that if for some reason we lose today, we'll have a chance to win again tomorrow. And we know that having it all means being able to see our lives in perspective.